A Time for Anger

BY FRANKY SCHAEFFER

Principal one-man shows (painting and/or graphics)

Frisch Gallery, New York, N.Y. (March 1970)
Garden Center, Tulsa, Oklahoma (February 1971)
Criteria Arts, London, U. K. (November 1972)
Galerie Chante-Pierre, Aubonne (Geneva), Switzerland
(1974–75)

Films

Created/produced *How Should We Then Live?* (10 Episodes)
(5 hrs., 16mm, color) 1974–75.
Screenplay by and directed *Whatever Happened to the Human
Race?* (5 Episodes) (5 hrs., 16mm, color) 1977–79.
Hosted and directed *Reclaiming the World, Conversations with
Francis and Edith Schaeffer.* (10 Episodes) (5 hrs., 16mm, color)
1980.
Screenplay by (with Harold Fickett) and directed *The Second
American Revolution.* (40 min., 35 mm, color) 1981–82.

Books

Co-author of *Plan for Action.* (Revell, 1980)
Addicted to Mediocrity. (Crossway, 1981)

A Time for Anger

The Myth of Neutrality

FRANKY SCHAEFFER

CROSSWAY BOOKS • WESTCHESTER, ILLINOIS
A DIVISION OF GOOD NEWS PUBLISHERS

Cover design by Ray Cioni/The Cioni Artworks. Cover illustration by
Pieter Breughel the Elder, The Blind Leading the Blind. Credit:
Scala/Editorial Photocolor Archives.

First printing, 1982
Second printing, 1982
Third printing, 1982
Fourth printing, 1982
Fifth printing, 1983
Sixth printing, 1984
Seventh printing, 1984

Printed in the United States of America.

Library of Congress Catalog Card Number
82-71981

ISBN 0-89107-263-2

The publisher would like to express appreciation for permission
to quote from the following:

"My Turn," by Rev. Jerry Falwell, copyright © 1981 by *Newsweek*, from September 21, 1981 issue.

"The Myopic Press," by Hodding Carter, copyright © 1981 by *Newsweek*, from December 7, 1981 issue.

In Search of History, by Theodore H. White, copyright © 1978 by author; used by permission of Harper & Row.

Article by Russ Pulliam, copyright © 1981 by *Indianapolis News*, from December 19, 1981 issue.

Article by William B. Provine, reprinted from *Hard Choices* (a magazine companion to the television series *Hard Choices*); used by permission of KCTS-TV, Seattle and William B. Provine.

Articles by Dexter Duggan, copyright © 1981 by *Moral Majority Report*, from August 24 and September 21 issues.

To My Parents, Francis and Edith Schaeffer

To my father:
A man of courage, conviction and Christian
principle, who has stood faithfully in a world of
cowardice and compromise.

To my mother:
A woman of vision, depth, and love, who has
courageously provided a bright spot of humanity for
her family and so many others.

Thank you both.

Contents

Acknowledgments

First, I would like to thank Genie, my wife, and my three children, Jessica, Francis, and John. By their very presence and love, they allow me to exercise my creative powers, such as they are, in an environment which turns my energies toward the causes of love, compassion, and beauty. Life would be bankrupt without them.

Friends have played a particular role in developing the ideas expressed in this book. Jim Buchfuehrer, my partner (producer) and friend, has contributed through his friendship, our many conversations together, and our film work.

Mr. Ray Cioni has proved himself a staunch ally and friend. His creativity is a daily inspiration, not to mention his stunning cover design for this book!

Thank you, Harold Fickett, for your excellent editorial work on this book. Thank you, too, for wise counsel and friendship.

Thanks, also, to Jerry Nims who has helped to forward the good cause, and my publishers, particularly Lane Dennis, for his support and encouragement.

John Whitehead holds a special place in my esteem, and I wish to thank him for his helpful suggestions on this book, and his friendship. Thank you, too, Cal Thomas, for all the good conversations and material which fed into this work.

This book is dedicated to my parents. It is written as well, however, for all those countless courageous Christians of strong principle and faith who refuse to be manipulated by the secular humanistic elite, now or ever. May God bless our efforts.

Author's Foreword

In the twentieth century, evangelical Christians in America have naively accepted the role assigned us by an anti-religious, anti-Christian consensus in society. We have been relegated to a cultural backwater, where we are meant to paddle around content in the knowledge that we are merely allowed to exist.

For those of us who would like to have an impact on our culture, and to those for whom "religious freedom" means more than the right to preach a shallow, simplistic gospel, this book may perhaps serve as a statement of purpose.

Four outstanding books have been written in the last decade which, taken together, provide the framework for this work. They are: *How Should We Then Live?* by my father, Francis Schaeffer; *Whatever Happened To The Human Race?* by Francis Schaeffer and C. Everett Koop, M.D. (Surgeon General of the United States); *A Christian Manifesto* by Francis Schaeffer; and *The Second American Revolution* by John W. Whitehead.

These four books set out the theological, philosophical, and historical underpinnings of our common vision. I trust, however, the perspective I offer here will add to the vision of those books and that which I have tried to share in my films and will broaden the understanding of Christians as to why and how they can challenge the superficial, glib, and anti-Christian stance of the pagan culture around us.

This book is not a treatise or great apologetic for the Christian faith. It is, however, a deeply felt statement about the bankruptcy of the human spirit in the age in which we live. If this volume starts even one or two Christians thinking of practical ways to stanch the flow of the twentieth century's self-righteous inhumanity, then it will have served its purpose.

History is made of ideas, and ideas are power.

Franky Schaeffer
1982

1 / The Basic Deception

There are times in which anyone with a shred of moral principle should be profoundly angry. We live in such times.

Our world is deeply deceitful. The "liberal," humanistic elements of American society do not play by the rules they espouse: the rules of open-mindedness, fair-play, and equality under the law.

Deceit and evil always go hand in hand, and our own age finds them wedded once more. For example, think of the abuse of language today. "Choice" has come to mean death. "Government assistance," control of the population. "Liberal," an indefinite tolerance of everyone and anything, *except* those who disagree about issues on the basis of moral principle. "Pluralism" no longer means that men may differ in their views of truth, but that truth does not really exist, outside the limited sphere of science.

Think of the use of labels to categorize political activity. Some labels are used to neutralize the actions of certain groups; others denote being "one of us," acceptable.

The words "right wing," "fundamentalist," "pro-life," "absolutist," and "deeply religious" are put-downs more than categories. Conversely, think of the unspoken pat on the back and blessing that the following words convey: "moderate," "pluralistic," "liberal," "civil libertarian," "pragmatic," and "enlightened."

Life, people, politics and social action cannot be reduced to one-word categories; when they are, falsehood and political manipulation become the norm. Mass media, by their very nature, must to a certain extent indulge in the shorthand of labels. But the deliberate abuse of labeling has conditioned the population to respond negatively to any mention of religious concern in the public sphere.

For instance, consider the following sentences. "Ms. Baker is a longstanding civil libertarian who, while personally opposed to abortion, is an advocate of pro-choice legislation, which would give each woman the right over her own body." Immediately we think of Ms. Baker as a young, trim, attractive woman; she has a first-rate education, knows all the right people in Washington, D.C.; she probably has an apartment in New York crammed with books and artwork and a record collection that includes Vivaldi and a complete set of Beatles albums. Perhaps she is the twin sister of the model used in the "You've come a long way, baby" cigarette ads.

Take, on the other hand, this sentence, "Mrs. Smith, the wife of Mr. Smith, a long-time right-wing activist, is profamily and a fundamentalist Christian." The image we automatically have of Mrs. Smith is of an earnest but misguided woman who, when she is not being bossed around by her husband or hanging up his polyester leisure suit, is busy dusting the knick-knacks she collected on their recent trip to Fort Lauderdale, Florida. In her spare time, she hands out leaflets which would curb all *our* civil rights.[1]

In essence, Mrs. Smith, while perhaps personally harmless, is clearly identified as "not one of us," or, in fact, "the enemy." The Mrs. Smiths of this world definitely should be kept down through ridicule. She is almost as legitimate an object of scorn as a member of the Klu Klux Klan.

Deceit always deals in stereotypes; and stereotypes perpetuate bigotry. The Indian as a "savage red man," the black person as a shuffling Uncle Tom, these images have been used in our nation's history to oppress and exploit minority groups. Hitler, in *Mein Kampf,* never dealt with any individual Jew, his family, his aspirations, his fears, his thoughts, or what he personally could contribute to society. He wrote only of the "Jewish race," in broad, general, and paranoid terms. Today, as Christians have declined in influence,[2] they have become subject to misrepresentation in similar ways. The secular humanist, although he would never dream of committing the social *faux pas* of calling a black man a Negro, feels perfectly free to castigate Christians and their leaders in any way he likes.

A vignette, taken from James Atlas's article about The American Writers Congress in the January 1982 issue of the *Atlantic,* shows how totally false many liberal secular humanists can be to their own supposed principles in this regard. Atlas describes a session of the Writers Congress on the topic: "The Book Wars: Local Censorship of Language and Ideas." One panelist, a representative from the Moral Majority, the Rev. H. Lamarr Mooneyham, attracted most of the crowd's "questions" and all of its ire. "Few people [in the crowd]," Atlas remarks, "had even seen such people." Nevertheless, they bombarded the Rev. Mooneyham with autobiographical statements and harangues.

> Deferential and articulate, the Moral Majoritarian was unnervingly reasonable in defending the right of creationists to protect their children from atheistic ideas; the liberal audience was intolerant and rude—self-righteous . . . ignoring the moderator's determined efforts to find out what the "question" was.

Many who work in mass media, with their secular humanist preconceptions, deny their true role; they consider themselves *objective reporters* who do not make value judgments. This is a total fiction. Elsewhere I have written about the "myth of neutrality," the ways of thinking by which secular humanists deceive themselves and others about the nature of their own beliefs.[3] Their pretense of objectivity contributes mightily to this "myth" or collective illusion.

To pursue how value judgments often enter into "objective reporting," let's compare two articles published in *Time* magazine. In their September 7, 1981 issue, a long article called "Cradle to Grave Intimacy" appeared. It was subtitled: "Some researchers openly argue that anything goes for children." The article revealed that "a disturbing idea is gaining currency within the sex establishment: very young children should be allowed, and perhaps encouraged, to conduct full sex life without interference from parents and the law." The article detailed how "sexologists" are urging that the final taboo in permissive sex— sex between adults and children—be broken down for everyone's good.

Time went on to decry this development and denounce it. They ended up quoting psychiatrist Edward Ritvo as saying, "Childhood sexuality is like playing with a loaded gun." This seemed to sum up what they felt about the whole thing. So far, so good. I couldn't agree more.

Several months earlier, however, in the April 6, 1981 issue, *Time* did a cover story on the issue of abortion. In that story they were careful to slant the entire article in favor of the "pro-choice" position. They ended that piece with a clear paragraph strongly endorsing legalized abortion; calling abortion a "question of conscience—inherently a personal matter," they went on to describe the pro-choice position as being "more in tune with the spirit of a pluralistic society" because it leaves abortion decisions up to individuals.

The discrepancy between the two articles shows clearly their duplicity and the impossibility of a consistent ethic without appealing to an objective standard. If *Time* and other mass media publications cannot stomach, quite yet that is, the idea of incest and the sexual abuse of children,[4] and feel compelled to denounce it, and yet urge a pluralistic, do-your-own-thing society when it comes to abortion, the ultimate child abuse, how can they pretend not to be arbitrating or deciding between competing values? (Remember, these articles were *not* editorials but "straight news" stories.)

And yet, hardly anyone challenges *Time* and other media, opinion-making institutions about their incredible double-standard, their on-again, off-again "morality."

Certainly the publications themselves never examine and state publicly their own moral criteria, or lack of them. They respond, willy-nilly, to the "temper of the times." As soon as some outrage becomes acceptable to a broad cross-section of people, or the "authorities" to whom the eastern press establishment looks—those scholars, politicians, and clergymen who are "moderate" and "progressive" and "pluralistic" (the same litany, with slight variations)—then all of a sudden a publication like *Time* changes course in midstream and acts as if nothing happened. Nowhere do they, or those like them, have the guts to face the real issue; that is, having denounced all absolute morality as "puritanical and oppressive," they never consider that *they* have no basis on which to make value judgments of any kind. Logically speaking, they should *welcome* with open arms all experimentation and such "innovations" as the sexual exploitation of children. After all, they have come to accept abortion and casual talk of euthanasia, so why stop there? But for them it's all a matter of responding, like chemicals in the presence of a catalyst, to the market place—not a matter of principle, not even of rigorous thinking.

Besides the way in which arbitrary value judgments insinuate themselves into the news, the "myth of neutrality" includes the widespread (often deliberate) misunderstanding of the separation of church and state. The Constitution separated the *institution* of the church from the state, but not a religious understanding of truth from the state. The further idea that citizens with religious convictions should disqualify themselves from any meaningful political activity, because of their so-called bias, is an utter contradiction of the First Amendment. The amendment provided freedom *for* religion, not freedom *from* religion.[5]

The Declaration of Independence, which sets out the philosophical framework within which the Constitution and the Bill of Rights are to be interpreted, justifies the American revolution *on religious grounds.* The colonists revolted because their "inalienable" (God-given) rights had been violated. They formed a new union which, by design, was to be in accord with the "laws of Nature and of Nature's God."

In addition, the basic legal framework of the United States was, until recently, based upon the traditional British common law, which looked to the Ten Commandments and biblical absolutes as its basis. Religious truth, specifically the Judeo-Christian tradition, was the ground on which the Republic stood.

Those who, like the ACLU, have authored the self-serving constitutional "re-write," and have revised American history in accord with their secularist views, have deliberately ignored these facts. Their teachings have produced an uneducated generation which firmly believes in a misbegotten notion of the separation between church and state. This misinformed secularist group then uses this lie to keep Christians and those with religious principles out of "the process," with the same mature logic of a two-year-old refusing to share his toys.

As an example, consider the effort to shunt the issue of abortion onto a siding and prevent it from becoming the *human rights* issue it truly is. By branding abortion a "Catholic" or "religious" issue, its advocates try to preclude a full discussion of the pro-life stance in the media.

And then its supporters refer to abortion as a "secular constitutional question," so that it will be handled exclusively by the courts (courts, moreover, which are controlled by secularist thinkers). Thus, they circumvent the democratic process and eliminate any chance for Christians to take a stand.

Another example would be the way in which figures like Jerry Falwell are often misrepresented and become the object of casual slurs in the press. Defending himself against this type of secularist bigotry, Falwell wrote in the "My Turn" section of *Newsweek,* September 21, 1981:

> "An unconditional right to say what one pleases about public affairs is what I consider to be the minimum guarantee of the First Amendment." The author of that remark was not a "right-wing, fundamentalist" preacher, but the late Supreme Court Justice Hugo Black.
>
> When liberals first began attacking the Moral Majority, they said we had no right to speak out. When it was pointed out that the liberal agenda was well represented in the 1960s and '70s in the government, in the streets and in liberal churches, the liberals conceded that while we had the right to speak, it was wrong for us to try to "impose" our moral viewpoint on everyone else.
>
> Of course, there was nothing wrong, so far as liberals were concerned, with "imposing" their own views, whether those views had to do with civil rights, the Vietnam War, busing, the eradication of voluntary school prayer or the extermination of unborn babies through abortion. Liberals could impose their views because liberals were right! And they call us arrogant! . . .
>
> It is not the religious conservatives in this country who have politicized the Gospel. It is the liberal in the church and in the government who has turned the basic moral values that were the foundation of this country into political issues. . . .
>
> Let's remember that all law is the imposition of someone's morality to the exclusion of someone else's morality. We have laws against murder, rape, incest, cannibalism

and stealing. No doubt, there are murderers, rapists, practitioners of incest, cannibals and thieves who are upset that their "rights" have been denied. But in order to provide for the common defense and promote the general welfare, it was deemed necessary to pass such laws.[6]

Talk about the division of church and state is often a red herring, a convenient excuse for muzzling undesirable opinion rather than a real concern on the part of the liberal, humanistic consensus.

The great danger of this thinking has been that, like all propaganda, it has been effective not only with those who otherwise would be neutral, but also, in some measure, with those on the other side. Those with strong religious convictions often have an inferiority complex, they are hesitant to express serious political concerns or opinions, let alone take action.

Again, take the issue of abortion. We have an array of Christian political figures who say publicly that, although they hold an antiabortion view themselves, they would not dream of "imposing" their view on society. We have been conditioned to see such statements as sensible and broad-minded. But would we expect that a feminist elected to office would say that, while she herself had strong, private proabortion views, she would in no way impose this secular, humanistic death-faith of hers on the citizenry in general? Strictures of this kind are never reciprocal; the feminist or any other lobbyist for some branch of secularism may freely use his or her position to influence the public or a governmental body, while the person of religious conviction, according to the new arbitrary rules, may not do so. *This is the myth of neutrality.*

It often seems as if only one point of view is given consistent exposure: the secular humanist point of view.[7]

George F. Will, in a *Washington Post* column, put it this way:

The idea that "freedom of choice" is necessarily neutral as regards social outcomes is the characteristic pretense of liberal societies. But liberal societies do not provide "freedom of choice" without having certain expectations about which choices will be made. And they try to shape choices by shaping attitudes. All societies do this. Only liberal societies pretend to be neutral.

The greatest danger we face in this era as Christians is from ourselves, not the opposition. If we accept the myth of neutrality, and its doctrine of our own one-sidedness, we will have abandoned our constitutional rights and, by default, lose our ability—more, *abdicated our commanded duty*—to be the "salt of the earth," the preservers of our culture.

If we had applied in the past the principles of Christian noninvolvement now being thrust upon us, we might have a flourishing slave trade today, as well as many other social iniquities that were abolished (or at least modified) by persons of great religious and moral convictions. Our Christian forebears deliberately acted upon their convictions to right the wrongs they perceived through public action, on the basis of religious faith.

While Christians, as all humans, have erred many times in their social attitudes, nevertheless, throughout history wherever true humanitarian stirrings occur, behind those stirrings there is a remarkable predominance of those who hold Jewish or Christian beliefs, or a conception of morality derived from these faiths. It is no accident that so many hospitals, orphanages, and other charitable endeavors worldwide were started by people who were deliberately acting on their Christian principles.

Every human being has a religion: he holds certain values, and these values imply a rationale; in this it makes no difference whether someone has accepted the values of an organized religion or has chosen his own. Everyone

believes in something, even if that "something" is his re-
pudiation of all organized religions. Although man is capable of dispassionate inquiry, there is, finally, no such
thing as a nonreligious view of truth: to value one thing as
opposed to another is to make a declaration of faith. All
life is religious, and all life is secular. There is no real
division between the two.

Professor Harvey Cox of the Harvard Divinity
School, in his book *The Secular City* (1965), writes that
secularism

> is not only indifferent to alternative religious systems, but
> as a religious ideology it is opposed to any other religious
> sytems. It is, therefore, a closed system.
>
> Secular humanism is a dangerous ideological system
> because it "seeks to impose its ideology through the organs
> of the State." Because secular humanism has no tolerance
> and is opposed to other religions, it actively rejects, ex-
> cludes and attempts to eliminate traditional theism from
> meaningful participation in the American culture.[8]

When Professor Cox uses the term "secular humanism," he does *not* refer to humanitarian endeavors, works
of charity. Nor does he refer to the study of the humanities, the academic disciplines which include the fine arts,
literature, language study, history and philosophy. Hu-
manitarianism and the study of the humanities are
obviously part of the church's mission. Secular humanism,
as Professor Cox uses the term and as I will employ it
throughout this book, is a philosophy which holds that
God is nonexistent or irrelevant to human affairs, and that
man must choose or invent his own ethics; secular humanism makes man the measure of all things. This philosophy
always seeks to exclude God from the discussion of moral
issues, and to do so, as Cox argues, puts it at loggerheads
with Christianity.

Everyone has some moral base, even if his "morality" is expressed in immorality or his faith is faith in not having any faith at all.[9] That those who do not hold traditional religious or moral positions are somehow operating from a more "neutral" and open-minded stance is illogical and preposterous, especially when seen in the light of the religious fervor with which they propagate their secularist position.

The person of religious conviction is no more biased than anyone else. He has the right to worship as he chooses, *and* he has the right, as does every other citizen, to engage in political and other human activities like everyone else, on the basis and *because of his principles and moral convictions*. He has the right to speak out, vote, and agitate for change as a Christian, just as the secular humanist has the right to speak out as a humanist.

All law is, in fact, some form of legislated morality. The question is whose morality will dominate. Laws against racial discrimination are legislated morality. So are the common laws against theft and murder. All of these laws "restrict" someone's choice, but are accepted as necessary to the common good.

It is therefore a lie and a deception to pretend that moral or religious views cannot be allowed to effect change. In fact, those who would silence the Christian political voice, the secular humanist elite, are attempting to impose *their* vicious version of morality on society, in direct contradiction to their arguments against political involvement by Christians. Worst of all, they are trying to prevent the issues from *even being discussed*. Unfortunately, they have been very successful. This must change. We must fight for the same rights of free speech and action as supposedly accorded *all* citizens.

2 / The Myth of Neutrality in the Media

In the United States today, and indeed in the whole world, one group more than any other forms public opinions: the media. The film industry, the television networks, newspapers, periodicals, and the people who run these enterprises have an immense amount of power, which is totally disproportionate to their numbers and, unhappily, to their moral perception and compassion.

Members of the media share a set of attitudes that can be characterized as "liberal" and "humanistic" in such overwhelming numbers that our sources of information have become utterly biased. In 1982, S. Robert Lichter and Stanley Rothman conducted hour-long interviews with 240 journalists and broadcasters at the most influential media outlets, including the *New York Times, Washington Post, Wall Street Journal, Time* magazine, *U. S. News & World Report,* CBS, NBC, ABC, PBS, and major public broadcasting stations.[1] The results of this survey are startling and confirm, even beyond one's worst suspicions, the religious commitment of the media to secular humanism.

"Ideologically," the author tells us, "a majority of leading journalists describe themselves as liberals. Fifty-four percent place themselves to the left of center, compared to only 19 percent who choose the right side of the spectrum." Those interviewed also generally agreed with the left's accusations about American foreign policy in the Third World.

"Fifty-six percent agree that American economic exploitation has contributed to Third World poverty . . . By
a 3-to-1 ratio, leading journalists reject the counterargu-
ment that Third World nations would be even worse off
without the assistance they've received from Western nations."

When the questions concerned the social issues of the
day, agreement among media members became greater
still.

"In their attitudes toward sex and sex roles, members
of the media elite are virtually unanimous in opposing the
constraints of both government and tradition. . . . Ninety
percent agree that a woman has the right to decide for
herself whether to have an abortion. Seventy-nine percent
agree strongly with this pro-choice position. . . . Fifty-
four percent do not regard adultery as wrong, and only 15
percent strongly agree that extramarital affairs are immor-
al."

The survey showed that members of the media know
how powerful they are. When asked to rank seven leadership groups, including black leaders, feminists, consumer
groups, intellectuals, labor unions, business leaders, and
the news media, they put themselves in the penultimate
position, second only in influence to business leaders. And
then, when asked who ought to have the most influence,
they put themselves first!

With such widespread agreement about basic issues,
which can only stem from the same philosophic outlook, it hardly takes a conspiracy for the media machine to speak with
one smothering voice. And these are those to whom we
must look for unbiased "reporting"![2] Given the concentration of the media's power in relatively few hands, and their
shared values, it's nearly impossible to avoid the conclusion that the media represent a monolithic, unelected force

in public life: a self-assured, self-perpetuating elite that relishes its power and would have more.

The most devastating fact which emerged from the survey still remains. In a nation in which seven out of ten Americans say they are church members and 60 percent claim that their religious beliefs are very important, 50 percent of those surveyed had no religious affiliation, and 86 percent *seldom* or *never* attend religious services. Little wonder that all things Christian in origin are routinely denigrated. In effect, the media have become the enemy of religious principle and also because of their vast unelected power, the rival of the constitutional process and of elected officials.

Granted, if the Christian is willing to stay in his little corner and do "religious activities" separated from the arts, industry, politics, science, law, economics, the media, or scholarship—in other words, all that really counts—then he is left to himself. As long as the Christian only sets out to convert souls, fine. But let him stand up and begin to challenge the dominant, humanistic forces and the press will make every attempt to either ignore or ravage that individual. As the Rev. Rousas John Rushdoony rightly says, "The evangelical impact on American politics in 1980 and 1981 stirs up daily wrath in the press and from politicians, because it reintroduces into politics a dimension which politicians largely have sought to avoid, moral confrontation. The hatred for all such evangelical groups is not because of their real or fancied blunders but because they have reintroduced biblical morality into politics" (from *Chalcedon Report,* No. 196, December 1981). The one thing the media abhor almost without exception is anyone who takes a firm stand on any issue out of religious principle, unless that stand happens to coincide with their expressed views.

A case in point is my friend, Dr. C. Everett Koop.

A little background is in order. In 1977 and '78, I

wrote the screenplay for and directed the five-hour documentary series, *Whatever Happened to the Human Race?* It featured as its narrators Dr. C. Everett Koop, then surgeon-in-chief of Philadelphia Children's Hospital and professor of pediatric surgery at the University of Pennsylvania, and Francis A. Schaeffer.

This film and its companion book investigated the disintegration of the West's view of man, as mirrored in the dramatic changes taking place in the realm of medical practice and ethics. Specifically, it dealt with how legalized abortion, a practice abhorred in every century from the time of the church fathers until our own, has transformed our society into one which not only tolerates abortion but also in many ways advocates it as a solution to social problems.

The project also included a close examination of a very real and often ignored fact of medical life today: infanticide. Infanticide is the killing of children *who have been born,* usually by deliberate neglect or lack of treatment in our hospitals, because they have some physical defect and so are considered "problem infants." Finally, the project examined the whole question of euthanasia. A growing, clamorous clique of "ethicists," whose views push what is morally acceptable to further and further inhuman limits, advocate doing away with the elderly, as we dispose of unwanted fetuses, when they become "too expensive." (End of background, now to my tale.)

A ninety-minute edited version of the series was shown in many cities in the United States. Channel 7, in Washington, D.C., decided to air the program in prime time.

Advance word of its broadcast got out via the fund-raising efforts of the small group of local Christians who were purchasing the time to have the show broadcast (you usually have to purchase time for programs from a Christian perspective). There was an immediate and shrill reaction from liberal organizations who espouse the "pro-choice" position on abortion. The Religious Coalition for Abortion Rights[3] sent a letter out to its members urging them to bombard Channel 7 with calls and letters demand-ing that they not even sell the time. (Strange behavior for "open-minded" liberals!) The letter castigated our show and branded it "propaganda." It also questioned the ethics of Channel 7 for being willing to show the program at all. (I thought liberals were against television censorship, but I guess not.)[4]

In due course, the program *was* aired, and was fol-lowed by a review on the second of January, 1981, by Judy Mann in the *Washington Post*. The headline of the article, "No Matter How Moving, Show Still Propaganda," basi-cally summed up her "neutral" point of view. The article itself began, "Score a resounding ten points on the emo-tional Richter scale for the anti-abortion forces that have produced a film *Whatever Happened to the Human Race?*" Parroting the Abortion Rights letter, the review went on to call Channel 7 to task for being willing to show a film that is "propaganda masquerading as public affairs pro-gramming." This would be a good slogan for PBS to adopt for itself. That is not, however, what she had in mind. The article concluded by quoting several executives of various proabortion organizations who questioned the accuracy of the show and insinuated that Francis Schaeffer must be a dark, cultish figure with such questions as ill-informed as, "Who is he, really?" Naturally, there were no quotes included from any of those involved in the making of this film, or from Dr. Koop or Francis Schaeffer, or, for that matter, *anyone at all* who took a prolife view.

A few weeks later, the second chapter in this story began with Dr. C. Everett Koop's appointment by the Reagan administration to the position of Deputy Assistant Secretary to Health and Human Services, putting him in line to become Surgeon General of the United States.

The *Washington Post,* in an article by Bill Peterson on March 6, 1981, headlined "Abortion Foes Gain Key Federal Posts," described Dr. Koop as "a leading anti-abortionist." The article's subtitle, "From Inside Administration, They Target Birth Control, Other Programs," summarizes the paper's tactics in its efforts to arouse the reader's opposition to these appointments. Ostensibly reporting on Dr. Koop's new post and that of Marjory Mecklenburg to that of head of the Office of Adolescent Pregnancy Programs, the article concentrated on alleged attacks against birth control programs by antiabortion groups. Dr. Koop was dispatched and dismissed with the following label: "A fundamentalist Christian with a Lincolnesque beard, Koop has been a board member of at least two anti-abortion groups—the National Right to Life Committee and the Americans United for Life—and is the narrator of a controversial anti-abortion film, *Whatever Happened to the Human Race?*"

One has to acknowledge that, given the mood of the country, Dr. Koop's antiabortion stand might well be the "hook" on which a journalist might hang his story. But the article, besides mentioning just once that Koop was "a Philadelphia surgeon," never explained what kind of surgeon, what posts Dr. Koop has held, or any of his other accomplishments. Also, in an article that concentrated on the status of birth control programs, the author never addressed the question of whether Dr. Koop believes in contraception (which he does). These deliberate omissions misrepresented Dr. Koop by lumping him together with anticontraception groups whose views he does not share, and by making it seem that his antiabortion stand was his sole qualification for the job of Surgeon General. This was not merely shoddy journalism; it was biased reporting with the purpose of arousing opposition to Dr. Koop's appointment; its propagandistic style is tantamount to character assassination.

One paragraph makes the motivation of the writer indisputable:

> Several pieces of legislation affecting family planning and world population control come up for renewal this year, and proponents are concerned, with the current emphasis on budget cutting, these programs may become expendable. There are some reassuring signs.

Now, why should the signs be "reassuring" unless the writer himself is a "proponent"? Whatever we may think about the issue itself, it is clearly not the role of an "objective reporter" to tell us which signs are reassuring and which are not. But the plain intent of the whole article is to alert the liberal populace that Reagan had the audacity to appoint people to government posts with views different from theirs, and to this end the author uses scare tactics and crucial omissions of a host of pointedly relevant facts.

How different the article would be if the author had mentioned that Dr. Koop was surgeon-in-chief of the Children's Hospital in Philadelphia, where the entire surgical center is named in his honor; that he is the inventor of many pediatric surgical techniques; that for his contributions to medical practice he has, among other awards, been made a member of the *Legion d'Honeur* by the French government; that he has pioneered and administered countless Third World medical relief efforts; and that he is the founder and was the editor-in-chief of the *Journal of Pediatric Surgery*. But no, he was simply branded an "anti-abortion activist," not "our" sort of person. Even in follow-up articles about Dr. Koop, most of his accomplishments were not mentioned, and his views were caricatured as extremist because the rationale behind them was never dealt with. His eventual confirmation as Surgeon General (by contrast) received scant attention. The public was left to draw the conclusion that lunatics must be running the government.

Other newspapers picked up the original *Post* story, and Dr. Koop's chief accomplishment in life, as far as they were concerned, seems to have been his activity on behalf of the unborn. (Not bad, if you ask me, but they didn't seem to like it.)

Eventually, *Time* magazine ran a story about Dr. Koop's nomination entitled, "Thunderings from the Right." (Their version of "The Peasants Are Coming!") In that article they referred to Dr. Koop as a doctor who, like some sideshow magician, had "made his name in the '70s separating Siamese twins." They also referred to the fact that he had appeared in the antiabortion "presentation" *Whatever Happened to the Human Race?* and let it go at that.

The *Boston Globe* dismissed Dr. Koop in an editorial as a mere "clinician . . . with tunnel vision."

Finally, the story eventually came to the attention of the lowest form of life involved in the business of selling information for profit: the network news. NBC prepared a special report for their weekend edition on Sunday, March 15, 1981, in which they featured Dr. Koop as a recent Reagan appointee and referred to him unflatteringly as someone who "had appeared in a prolife propaganda film." NBC could not bring themselves to mention the name of the film, anything about it, or *any* of Dr. Koop's credentials. It seems that the only point they felt they wanted to borrow conveniently from the *Washington Post* article was that he was somehow involved in "propaganda."[5]

When news organizations can misrepresent a man to this extent and with a single voice, when they are interested in a Dr. Koop only insofar as they can ignore his credentials and belittle and snipe at him for being a physician who is acutely aware that human life is sacred, special, beautiful, then we have to draw our own conclusions about "propaganda."

Note how small and incestuous the media world is.

Once one member approaches a story in a certain way, there is little chance that the tone taken by other major news conglomerates will be any different.

Hodding Carter, chief correspondent and anchorman for the PBS series "Inside Story," recently took his colleagues to task, in an essay published in *Newsweek,* for listening only to the voices of the "established mainstream." He stated his opinion that, when it comes to being heard by the media, the culturally disenfranchised (i.e., the evangelical world) and those seeking to change society "might as well be inhabitants of a far-off planet." And then he focused on what this means in terms of the status of the media as a social institution and its role:

> To put it another way, American journalism is an extremely prosperous, extraordinarily comfortable and dangerously smug player in the upper reaches of the establishment power game. Our editorial pages and commentaries reflect a range of opinion from A to B. The unspoken as well as explicit assumptions of the society are the unspoken and unchallenged assumptions of the media. . . .
>
> An unfair indictment? No. It is, if anything, understated. The press of America, print and broadcast, has been blind for decades to each new gathering storm. The black revolution, the feminist revolt, the fundamentalist Christian backlash—none was anticipated by the press and none was well understood or well covered in its early stages. When each mass phenomenon's insistence and power were finally too visible to be ignored, each was covered in familiar ways whose effect was to minimize its depth and breadth and so categorize its leadership and goals as to caricature both.[6]

Hodding Carter's remarks might be thought to be self-contradictory: if the press were really so prejudiced, why then would an establishment magazine like *Newsweek* give his opinions a forum? Carter himself, though, notes that criticism, when it is allowed, usually comes from "in-house radicals," kept around much as certain corporations tolerate a token black or two to enhance their image.

When others challenge the media, especially in dramatic and effective ways, they respond with the kind of anger that, like some great sleeping sow that has been prodded into grumbling wakefulness, exposes their bigotry and makes them look just plain stupid. Those of us in the evangelical world, suffering as we do from a cultural inferiority complex, might be tempted to accept passively the way in which Dr. Koop was treated, as a sort of inevitable consequence of his evangelical faith. And I might be accused of over-reacting because Dr. Koop is my friend.

But there is one case amongst many that proves definitively that *any* Christian,[7] from whatever branch of the church, will be rhetorically drawn and quartered if he speaks out effectively against the media or their cherished views. In 1978 Aleksandr Solzhenitsyn was invited to give the Commencement speech at Harvard University. It had been many years since the voice of truth had spoken out at Harvard with such eloquence, and the audience gave him a standing ovation. He criticized the West for its materialism and moral poverty. Tracing the advent of the West's "despiritualized and irreligious humanistic consciousness" back to the Renaissance and the Enlightenment, he showed that without the Christian understanding of man as a fallen creature, one in need of God's grace, the West has produced legalistic and degraded nations and cultures. And in this fine and rousing statement he pointed to the media as agents which have fostered this decline:

> The press too, of course, enjoys the widest freedom. (I shall be using the word press to include all media.) But what sort of use does it make of this freedom?
>
> . . . What sort of responsibility does a journalist have to his readers, or to history? If he has misled public opinion

or the government by inaccurate information or wrong conclusions, do we know of cases where the same journalist or the same newspaper has publicly recognized and rectified such mistake? No, it does not happen, because it would damage sales. . . .

How many hasty, immature, superficial, and misleading judgments are expressed every day, confusing readers, without any verification? The press can both stimulate public opinion and miseducate it. Thus we may see terrorists turned into heroes, or secret matters pertaining to one's nation's defense publicly revealed, or we may witness shameless intrusion on the privacy of well known people under the slogan: "Everyone is entitled to know everything." But this is a false slogan, characteristic of a false era: people also have the right not to know, and it is a much more valuable one. The right not to have their divine souls stuffed with gossip, nonsense, vain talk. A person who works and leads a meaningful life does not need the successive burdening flow of information.

Hastiness and superficiality are the psychic diseases of the twentieth century, and more than anywhere else this disease is reflected in the press. In-depth analysis of a problem is anathema to the press. It stops at sensational formulas.

Such as it is, however, the press has become the greatest power within the western countries. More powerful than the legislature, the executive, and judiciary. One would then like to ask: By what law has it been elected and to whom is it responsible? . . .

Enormous freedom exists for the press—but not for the readership, because newspapers mostly give stress and emphasis to those opinions which do not too sharply contradict their own, or the general trend.

Without any censorship, fashionable trends of thought and ideas in the West are carefully separated from those which are not fashionable; nothing is forbidden, but what is not fashionable will hardly ever find its way into periodicals or books or be heard in the colleges. Legally, your researchers are free, but they are conditioned by the fashion of the day. There is no open violence such as in the

east; however, a selection dictated by fashion and the need
to match mass standards frequently prevents independent-
minded people from giving their contribution to public
life. There is a dangerous tendency to form a herd, shut-
ting off successful development. . . .

After suffering decades of violence and depression, the
human soul longs for higher things, warmer and purer
than those offered by today's mass living habits, exempli-
fied by the revolting invasion of publicity, by TV stupor,
and by intolerable music. . . .

How did the media react to Solzhenitsyn's speech?
Did they take it as a tonic, a needed correction to one-sided
thinking? If anyone speaking in behalf of spiritual values
might have been heard, it would have been Solzhenitsyn.
He was the media's darling; a Nobel Prize winner, the
defender of free speech, and the most celebrated literary
man to emerge from Russia in the second half of the twentieth century, journalists had, until this time, presented
him as a living icon of every cherished western value.

The *New Yorker,* in their August 21, 1978 issue,
summarized the media's reaction in their "Notes and
Comment" section, without any attempt at so-called
liberal-minded fairness.

> While Alexander Solzhenitsyn remained in the Soviet
> Union,[8] it was possible for us in the United States to re-
> gard him as a marvelously steadfast believer in political
> freedom, but now that we have him in our midst, airing
> his views on American politics and American society, we
> have had to review our impressions.
>
> We find that primarily he is the champion not of free-
> dom but of spiritual well-being. The two causes are by no
> means the same. . . .

Olga Carlisle, writing in *Newsweek,* July 24, 1978,
said that Solzhenitsyn's "convictions are deeply rooted in
the Russian spirit, which is untempered by the civilizing

influences of a democratic tradition." Let's change that last sentence slightly and see how it sounds. What if we said, "Billy Sundance's convictions are deeply rooted in the American Indian spirit, which is untempered by the civilizing influences of a democratic tradition." What self-respecting secular humanist would say that? No one. You can't call an American Indian a barbarian (thankfully), but you can say anything about a Christian.

And the press did say just about anything and everything in reactionary rebuttal to Solzhenitsyn's arguments. Henry Fairlie in *The New Republic,* July 29, 1978, depicted Solzhenitsyn as a deranged man with a messiah complex living in a facsimile of a Gulag prison built to his order in Vermont. About his speech, Fairlie said, "There is nothing new in all of this—it is just the traditional voice of Russian authoritarianism and Orthodoxy—and there is nothing for the West to learn from it."

Hans J. Morgenthau, writing in the *New Leader,* July 3, 1978, felt compelled to trot out the most puerile, hackneyed, revisionist response to a Christian intellectual:

> He [Solzhenitsyn] reveals himself as a typical political romantic who tries to escape from the unresolved problems of the present into a Golden Age of the past that has never existed. One need only compare the Dark Ages with the subsequent Enlightenment to see how unreal his juxtapositions are. If they had a choice, how many people would prefer to continue living in the Dark Ages rather than enjoy the intellectual, social and political fruits of the Enlightenment?

Oh yes! The Dark Ages! The Spanish Inquisition! The Crusades! That's all there was of Christian civilization, right? Mr. Morgenthau needed his freshman political science teacher to point out to him that the Dark Ages resulted from the *pagan* destruction of the Roman Empire. Who brought us out of the Dark Ages? The Church. What about Rembrandt, Bach, Shakespeare, Martin Luther, Milton, Lincoln, parliamentary government, hospitals, orphanages, etc.? Or do none of these figure in today's history books? If it had been up to the Morgenthaus of the world, the Visigoths, with their "free and liberated" morality, would have converted the Empire to their ways, not vice versa. Raw meat, anyone? To put it another way, who, if they had the choice, would prefer the idle ravings of the "enlightened" Morgenthaus to the merciful actions of the "unenlightened" Mother Theresas?

In essence, the major news organizations of the United States do not represent what can be called a free press. A free press requires the presence of organizations which compete not merely to see whether CBS, NBC, or ABC can predict the outcome of an election thirty seconds ahead of its sisters, but organizations which represent *distinctly and substantially different points of view*. The shared humanistic consensus of *all* the major news organizations controls the "free flow of ideas" in our press almost as surely as the Communist Party controls the Soviet press. The Soviet press dispatches those whom it dislikes with epithets (and epitaphs) such as "antisocial" and "counter-revolutionary." The monolithic U.S. press performs a similar social service by labeling people "fundamentalist," "prolife," "devoutly Catholic," and "right wing." To say this is not to devalue the need of a free press, and no one should construe these remarks to mean that the press should be censored. Quite the contrary; by *demanding* the Christian voice be fairly heard, I am saying that the "philosophical censorship" of today's press must be lifted in order to rescue the institution of the press itself.

The massive power of the secularist absolutist media must not be underestimated. As media analysts so well understand, reality is often a state of mind inasmuch as the *way* something is reported determines in large measure *what* is reported. The liberal, humanistic press, by the selections it makes as to what to report and its decisions about how to report it, manipulates the news, pushing its version of "reality." This is why they routinely play down traditional religious people and ideas and play up secularist thinking, glossing over its glaring inadequacies and massive failures.[9] Leopold Tyrmand, in his essay, "The Media As Present Danger," cites an article in the *New York Times* which shows how the media will not admit to mistakes and will perpetuate them in order not to undercut their credibility.[10] A book called *Open Marriage* originally received "ecstatic publicity and the *Times* contributed mightily to its success." The book recommended infidelity as a remedy to personal and social problems. The *Times* article in question found the book's authors being interviewed several years after its publication. They "admitted that their recipe for easy happiness had failed, that many of those who tried it had ruined their lives." There was no call, however, on anyone's part for a return to traditional morality. The authors concluded only that their message was not for the masses, but for an elite; "in their perception, it was not the rottenness of their theorizing but their victims' lack of sophistication which was at fault" (p. 10). They failed to mention, however, that their book had been designed for the masses so it would sell. No one pointed this out, although the interview format certainly gave the writer ample opportunity to do so. The question, Tyrmand says, is, "Why does the *Times* once again advertise them in an interview filled with catchy platitudes and phrased with sympathy and quasi-objectivity, thereby compounding the original offense?"

An even more flagrant abuse of the media's power occurs when a news organization moves from being a news reporter to a newsmaker. An instance of this occurred during the *Whatever Happened to the Human Race?* seminar at Madison Square Garden in New York City.[11]

Inside the hall we had approximately one thousand

people who were spending two days watching a serious film and hearing lectures and discussions on the subjects of abortion, infanticide, and euthanasia. These were concerned people from all walks of life, a true cross-section, who were difficult to stereotype and therefore difficult to put in the appropriate media pigeon hole of "prolife activists" (who the media prefer to characterize as senile retired nuns!).

Outside the seminar hall on the sidewalk, there was a group of twelve people (I counted them) who arrived to picket the proceedings within as being "antichoice" and therefore dangerous.

"Coincidentally," they arrived and unpacked their four or five well-worn "prochoice" placards at the same time as a television truck arrived from the local news and a photographer arrived from the *Village Voice,* as well as some other media persons. Their picketing lasted for the exact amount of time it took the television truck to unpack its cameras, film them for a minute or so, and for the anchor person to do her "wrap-up" (twenty seconds) on the story.

The television cameras and the "reporter" never ventured into the auditorium, much less asked any of us, the organizers, what we were doing and saying, why one thousand people were inside talking and watching movies for two days. The three-minute "protest" was the story; the seminar itself was merely a footnote to be added to the framework for the predetermined story itself, which was, in essence, an event showing the onward march of the fashionable feminist-led proabortion movement. The media's posture of neutrality can hardly be maintained when it transforms the news into theatre *which it produces.*[12]

The media's growing mania for power and their discrimination against Christians and traditional Judeo-Christian ethics only represent one portion of their current deception. Since the ideology of the media is generally to the left of center politically (as we saw in the study cited herein), political conservatives and traditionalists also come in for their routine share of abuse.

The magazine *TV Guide* can hardly be considered an outspoken opponent of television and the media! Nevertheless, the May 29, 1982 issue of *TV Guide* did an exposé on one of the many campaigns of network television to target and destroy an individual or group. In this case, the article was called "Anatomy of a Smear (How CBS Broke the Rules and 'Got' General Westmoreland)." This "documentary," said *TV Guide,* began with the following statement:

> "Tonight we're going to present evidence of what we have come to believe was a conscious effort—indeed, a conspiracy—at the highest levels of American military intelligence to suppress and alter critical intelligence on the enemy in the year leading up to the Tet Offensive."

TV Guide went on to say,

> Thus, on the evening of January 23, 1982, CBS News, correspondent Mike Wallace, introduced a 90-minute documentary titled, "The Uncounted Enemy: A Vietnam Deception." What followed was a powerful and polished examination of a sensitive chapter in our recent history. Using the compelling testimony of ex-military officers, the program attacked the reputation of General William Westmoreland, the former Commander of the U.S. Military Forces in Vietnam. The evidence amassed by CBS seemed to prove the U.S. military intelligence operation in Vietnam, led by General Westmoreland, conspired to deceive President Lyndon Johnson, the Congress and the American public.

The article then goes on and does an exposé on the "exposé." It found the following "journalistic techniques" were used: formulating a thesis (that a conspiracy had been perpetrated) and then ignoring evidence which suggested otherwise; rehearsing with a paid consultant before interviewing him on the air; screening for a sympathetic witness; asking friendly witnesses soft questions but grilling unfriendly witnesses mercilessly; presenting quotes out of context, etc.

TV GUIDE then goes on in a lengthy article to carefully document its charges as listed above. At the end of the article the magazine makes the following statement:

> The network's lapses in the making of this documentary also raised larger questions. Are the network news divisions, with their immense power to influence the public's idea about politics and recent history, doing enough to keep their own houses in order? If this documentary is any evidence, then the answer may be No. The inaccuracies, the distortions, and the violations of journalistic standards in "The Uncounted Enemy" suggests that television news' "safeguards" for fairness and accuracy need tightening, if not wholesale revision.

And yet, journalists such as those mentioned in CBS seem to portray themselves as somehow benign public servants whose only interest in life is the public good. A description perhaps nearer the mark would be of men greedy for power, resentful of all those who stand in their way, and dedicated to their own philosophical point of view. In addition, one must realize that sensationalism and disproportion being the base upon which they draw large audiences, their own earnings (which are themselves enormous and disproportionate to their labors) would be in jeopardy if careful and reasoned analysis was their approach. Therefore, in considering the media's power and their routine denigration of Christians, it is well to remember that this is part of an even wider problem of the irresponsibility which follows the rejection by the media at large of moral absolutes and fixed standards by which to judge *their own behavior*—not to mention the behavior of others they supposedly are reporting on.

With the clever manipulation of questions, even the most "objective facts" from opinion polls, which the television networks are so fond of, can turn out to be not objective at all.

Consider, for instance, this question: "Do you oppose abortion on all grounds at any time?" Not even a majority of the prolife movement would answer this question affirmatively, because if the life of the mother were truly threatened (an instance that is very rare indeed), they would not oppose abortion. Therefore, a news organization could issue the following statement: "According to a recent poll, 88 percent of the American public polled do not oppose abortion." But if this question were asked, "Do you oppose permissive abortion-on-demand by anyone for any reason, of any age, with or without the consent of parents for teenagers, and in most cases for mere reasons of convenience up to the twenty-fourth week of pregnancy and often beyond?" then the statistics would show the public being against abortion. (The second question accurately reflects what abortion, in fact, has become. And, according to Joan Beck, in an article entitled, "Dr. Jekyll or Mr. Hyde? The Dilemma of Abortion" up to 80 percent *do* oppose abortion when the question addresses the current practice of abortion-on-demand.)

It is time to shed the naive idea that modern media exist only to perpetuate the free flow of information and the right of free speech. These multinational corporate news machines, along with their liberal establishment collaborators, exist to perpetuate themselves and their view of the world at all costs. Period. As Mr. Tyrmand says: "Does the press really care about what people are entitled to know? Or does it want merely to let people know what the media have said, and remember that it was the media who said it?" [*Rockford Papers*, p. 4].

To be fair, there have been voices raised within the press establishment itself recognizing some problems related to those raised in this book. However, the fact that a few lone voices speak out does not mean that anything will change. Indeed, up to the present the one or two that have spoken out within the press establishment have not been given much of a greater hearing than those of us who have spoken outside of it.

An example of someone who has spoken up is Mr. O'Neill, Editor of the *New York Daily News*. In his speech, given to the American Society of Newspaper Editors on May 5, 1982 (printed in *The Wall Street Journal* May 6), he said, among other things,

> While there has been an astonishing growth in the power of the media over the last decade or so, I am by no means sure that we are using it wisely. The tendency has been to revel in the power and wield it freely, rather than accept any corresponding increase in responsibility.
>
> The extraordinary powers of the media, most convincingly displayed by network TV and the National Press, have been mobilized to influence major public issues and national elections, to help diffuse the authority of Congress and to disassemble the political parties—even to make presidents or to break them. Indeed, the media now weighs so heavily in the scales of power that some political scientists fear we are upsetting the checks and balances invented by our forefathers.
>
> . . . Have we become so arrogant with our power, so competitive, that we cannot decide that the public crime is often not worth the private punishment? That the first amendment is often abused rather than served by those who would defend it?
>
> . . . We undermine public confidence and, without intending it, become a cause rather than just a reporter of national decline.

How long can we, as Christians, afford to underwrite with our subscription dollars and viewing habits these vast media empires? How long will Christians tolerate the bigotry and discrimination against themselves, against the sane compassionate view that *all* life is precious?

It is time for journalism to become a Christian mission field. Time for Christian writers to transform this monolithic system from within and restore truth to the machinery of the press. Time for more Christians to be in journalism school and fewer in Bible school. Time for those Christians in the media to stand up and push their own agenda with conviction.

It is time for us to overwhelm news organizations with calls, mail, and cancelled subscriptions at every fresh manifestation of anti-Christian bigotry and intolerance. Time for us to demand that the Judeo-Christian tradition be presented as an alternative whenever moral issues are raised. And it is time that Christian money be used to acquire news organizations and use them to editorialize for justice and life. It is time to buy up every new technology, cable system, UHF, satellite network, etc., and *fight for truth through all these media.*

In Yad Vashem, the Israeli memorial to the victims of the holocaust, there is a special monument to the Polish Jews who resisted the Nazis by fighting street by street in the Warsaw ghetto. It is time that we as Christians begin to make our stand while there are still battles that can be won.

3 / St. Peter, St. John, and Mother Theresa Versus the Boston Globe

In the September 27, 1981 *Boston Globe* magazine, an article about public professions of faith by George V. Higgins, a lawyer and columnist for the *Globe,* appeared. This article, "When Religion Goes Public," written in the tone of "light comedy," reveals far more about secular attitudes toward religion than its author probably intended.

> There is something about an unsolicited public profession of deep religious faith that sets the teeth on edge. Almost invariably the professor is up to something that will turn out to be extremely disagreeable for everybody else. More offensive still, he is usually visibly glad of it and does not even bother to pretend otherwise. . . .
>
> . . . The late Bishop Fulton Sheen, by all accounts a good and decent shepherd of his flock when he was tending it and not imitating Bob Hope armed with a mitre, was a fertile source of such mortification. . . .
>
> . . . Preposterous people often go to church and temple, and there isn't any way to keep them out, any more than there is any legal means of compelling the Reverend Jerry Falwell to undergo the laryngectomy that would do so much to improve life in this republic for the rest of us. . . .
>
> . . . Well, maybe centuries of silence constitute the best possible preparation for a dignified discussion of one's religious faith. . . .
>
> . . . It would be nice if all clergymen were like unto the Trappists. . . .[1]

We have to see first that Mr. Higgins has the common prejudice of many secular people, that religion, specifically Christianity, consists only of negative commandments, which serve only to make people unhappy. Now, it's true that Christians have at times turned the good news into an uncompromising set of legalisms. And we have to repent of this. But we must also see that Mr. Higgins and those who are like-minded want to associate Christianity exclusively with the dark moments of the Church's history and quite skillfully overlook the overwhelming evidence of the good people and work which Christianity has produced throughout the course of western civilization (which has, for one thing, been around longer than the *Boston Globe,* and presumably will survive it!).

Occasionally, by contrast to Mr. Higgins, a secular commentator will stumble upon a scene of Christian compassion, and the effects of this should teach us how important it is to reassert the role Christianity has played in culture and to reestablish that role. Teddy White can best be described as an agnostic. While traveling in China as a reporter for *Time* magazine, he witnessed the great Honan Famine which took place during World War II. His observations, which I will quote here, serve as a good example of the charity which Christians and Christianity have, for centuries, represented across the world.

> I was glazed with the sight when I arrived in Loyang, the provincial capital of Honan; and there at the station, in the dark, they were packing refugees into boxcars like lumber, stacking them together so they could not move, cursing them aboard the car roofs, with fathers hauling children up by the hand, dangling like packages, as they swung aloft for the night run over the gap. And again, the stink of urine and bodies; then through the deserted streets to the Catholic mission.
>
> Its master was Bishop Tomas Megan, of Eldors, Iowa, a stocky, cheerful, healthy man, devoutly Catholic and American. I learned in the next two weeks that he was

not only a good man but an effective one, for he was my thread to the Christian missionaries, and the Christian missions were the only connection to reason as I understood it. The Christian missionaries had come to spread the gospel—in rivalry. But buried in the gospel is a message of kindness. Now, in this theater of death, the missionaries were partners in charity, Americans joining with Europeans, Catholics with Protestants. Megan was Irish-American Catholic; two Italian Catholics, Father Fraternelli and Dr. Danielli, were his liaison in Chengchow; and though Americans and Italians were killing each other in Europe, here in Honan they were united in charity. In Chengchow, the Italian Catholics were joined by Mr. Ashforth, an American fundamentalist, in their hopeless struggle against desolation. What outside relief came in, came through the missionaries; and where we located them on our travels they were beleaguered, with crowds around the mission compounds, children and women sitting at their gates, babies dumped each morning at their threshold to be gathered in makeshift orphanages. Missionaries left their compounds only when necessary, for a white man walking in the street was the only agent of hope, and was assailed by wasted men, frail women, children, people head-knocking on the ground, groveling, kneeling, begging for food, wailing, *"K'o lien, k'o lien"* ("Mercy, mercy") but pleading really only for food. The handful of missionaries who staked out the Christian underground in the area of famine were the only thread of sense—the sense that life is precious.[2]

Teddy White can hardly be described as a biased propagator of the Christian faith! Nevertheless, he was so struck by what he saw in the charity of the missions that a few pages later in the book he states that he joined the Catholic missionary at Mass.

· Of course today we might talk of Christian efforts with Cambodian refugees, and in Somalia, and in every American city through the Salvation Army, the prolife movement, etc. So whenever we meet the prejudice of a

Mr. Higgins who thinks that Christians are only out to be "extremely disagreeable for everybody else," we must, out of compassion, refute this perverted notion and marshal the evidence of Christian centuries with their, in Solzhenitsyn's words, "great reserves of mercy and sacrifice."

In addition, we must harbor no illusions about the neutrality of social observers like Mr. Higgins; changing their minds will not simply be a process of jogging their historical memories; after all, one assumes they have access to libraries. They actively *do not want* to know the truth. Imbued with the antireligious bigotry of total secularism, they will naturally not take kindly to the Solzhenitsyns of the world who proclaim the truth of God's law and the salvation of Jesus Christ. I'm sure someone like Mr. Higgins regards himself as a "sane, middle-of-the-road liberal pragmatist," a keeper of the "tolerant, pluralistic faith." But the pretense of tolerance wears exceedingly thin when such tolerance suggests that it would be a good idea to cut someone's vocal cords out to silence them! Oh yes, Mr. Higgins' talk of a laryngectomy for Jerry Falwell is a piece of hyperbole, but by their metaphors ye shall know them! Basically, so many who supposedly champion the cause of free speech detest Christianity—it's a nightmare for them from which, they are at pains to assure themselves, history has finally awakened—and they never seriously consider admitting that its claims are worthy of scrutiny, let alone that it has produced anything of worth.

Such arrogant intolerance of those who wish to obey Christ's command to tell the good news and practice his teachings is not new. In the Book of Acts, chapter 4, we read:

> The priests and the captain of the temple guard and the Sadducees came up to Peter and John while they were speaking to the people. They were greatly disturbed because the apostles were teaching the people. . . .

They seized Peter and John and, because it was evening, they put them in jail until the next day. . . .

They had Peter and John brought before them and began to question them. . . .

When they saw the courage of Peter and John and realized that they were unschooled, ordinary men, they were astonished. . . .

So they ordered them to withdraw from the Sanhedrin and then conferred together. "What are we going to do with these men?" they asked. "Everybody living in Jerusalem knows they have done an outstanding miracle, and we cannot deny it. But to stop this thing from spreading any further among the people, we must warn these men to speak no longer to anyone in his name. . . ."

Then they called them in again and commanded them not to speak or teach at all in the name of Jesus. But Peter and John replied, "Judge for yourselves whether it is right in God's sight to obey you rather than God. For we cannot help speaking about what we have seen and heard."

In this passage we find guidance in how to answer a Mr. Higgins, a *Boston Globe,* a federal court, an IRS official, the ACLU, or whoever else wishes to stifle the voice of the gospel or the freedom to preach it, and, more importantly, apply its teachings in real life. Peter and John were arrested and persecuted not only for teaching but for the audacity of practicing that teaching in healing a crippled man outside of the normal practices of the day. In other words, they had cut across the path of the religious and secular leaders of their state, and, when challenged, refused to back down on the basis that God's law must be obeyed before man's law.

Upon their release, Peter and John went back to their own people and repeated all that the chief priests and elders had said to them. Then they prayed and worshipped together, and during that time Peter quoted the Psalmist: "Why do nations rage and the people plot in vain? The kings of the earth take their stand and the rulers gather together against the Lord and against His anointed one."

The psalmist's question, repeated by Peter after his arrest, should be ours today. "Why do the nations rage and the people plot in vain?" Our faith has the answer: man's rebellion against God. Further, the answer is contained again in the Psalms: "The fool has said in his heart, there is no God." Unhappily, so many Christians understand this only in theological terms. When faced with the deadly opposition of the secular world on social and cultural issues, and particularly when that opposition takes the form of the myth of neutrality, we often fail to recognize naked, intolerant evil for what it is. And, further, to realize that the elite which governs is often made up of the very "fools" the psalmist describes.

We can take hope in knowing that Christians have faced this opposition in every century since the birth of Christ; but we must also remind ourselves to make an appropriate response, as did Peter and John. When the Sanhedrin asked Peter and John, in so many words, why they were trying "to impose their religion on the Jerusalem community," their reply was that when it came to preaching God's Word or applying His teachings, they would not bow, in any way, to the secular-religious powers of that day. In other words, they thumbed their noses at their intolerant accusers.

As if to emphasize this point, in chapter 5 of Acts we read of yet another run-in with the law.

> Then the high priest and all his associates, who were members of the party of the Sadducees, were filled with jealousy. They arrested the apostles and put them in the public jail. But during the night an angel of the Lord opened the doors of the jail and brought them out. "Go, and stand in the temple court," he said, "and tell the people the full message of this new life."
>
> At daybreak they entered the temple courts, as they had been told, and began to teach the people. . . .

Then someone came and said, "Look! The men you put in jail are standing in the temple courts teaching the people." At that, the captain went with his officers and brought the apostles. They did not use force, because they feared that the people would stone them.

Having brought the apostles, they made them appear before the Sanhedrin to be questioned by the high priest. "We gave you strict orders not to teach in this name," he said. "Yet you have filled Jerusalem with your teaching and are determined to make us guilty of this man's blood."

Peter and the other apostles replied: "We must obey God rather than men!" . . .

When they heard this, they were furious and wanted to put them to death. . . .

The apostles left the Sanhedrin, rejoicing, because they had been counted worthy of suffering disgrace for the name. Day after day, in the temple courts and from house to house, they never stopped teaching and proclaiming the good news that Jesus is the Christ.

Peter and John's numerous brushes with the law and the nights they spent in jail emphasize how ready they were to stand up to the religious and civil authorities of the day, even to participate in civil disobediences if necessary. They knew what jail was like and they *kept going back* there for the sake of truth.

In reading the passages in Acts 5 about Peter's arrest, note that "they did not use force, because they feared that the people would stone them." The public support of those they had converted played a part in saving the lives of Peter and John. At that point they had converted about five thousand people and these followers in the city of Jerusalem provided enough public support that the Sanhedrin could not take these apostles quietly aside and "cut out their vocal cords" or put them to death.

A Mr. Higgins or a New York *Times* or a Supreme Court judge ought to be made acutely aware of the contemporary Christians who will not let them get away with silencing our voice.

Perhaps this story of Peter and John should be updated for our situation today. It might well read: "They did not use force, and were not able to eliminate the Christian witness, because they realized that the subscriptions to their newspaper would be cancelled if they kept up their anti-Christian barrage of propaganda. They were not able to do away with the Christian influence in their society because they realized they would lose the next election, their companies would be picketed, their secularized public schools abandoned, their court rooms deluged with suits, their abortion mills burned to the ground, and the nation would be brought to a standstill."

There is often a price to be paid, and we should be realistic about this. We read of Peter, "They called the apostles in and had them flogged. Then they ordered them not to speak in the name of Jesus and let them go." But notice what Peter and John did. With their backs still painfully tender, the blood scarcely dry from the flogging they had received, *they went straight out and disobeyed the state and courts of their day*. And "day after day, in the temple and courts from house to house, they never stopped teaching and proclaiming the good news that Jesus is the Christ." This is not pious irrelevant spiritual action. This is revolution.

We must develop this militant indifference to the edicts of mere men when they contradict God's law. We must emulate the courageous "Here I stand" attitude of Martin Luther.[3]

When it comes to preaching the gospel, we must also remember that the simple freedom to pass out a tract is not what is at stake. The devious, anti-Christian spirit of our age has taken a different form than it assumed in the age of the apostles. Our governing elite would, for the time being, allow us to preach the gospel. But they increasingly resist the application to our culture of the merciful teachings of our God, the author of all life. We must stand against this with the very same firmness with which the apostles stood against not being allowed to teach, heal, and congregate.

After all, what is the use of being allowed to preach a gospel that one is not allowed to practice? What is the use of telling how Jesus Christ affirmed our life in the flesh, if the life of our neighbors, the unborn in our own country, is not protected? What is the use of preaching a gospel and spreading the teachings of Christ when that gospel and those teachings are seen as irrelevant to the way in which we value life, to the issues of infanticide and euthanasia? What is the use of being allowed to preach such a "gospel" if it no longer contains good news for the defenseless? If it is no longer to be allowed to provide a sure humane moral base for education?

We must be willing to follow the example of St. Stephen. The martyr's concluding remarks as he faced the hostile, bigoted, antireligious authorities of his day *were far from words of acquiescence or complacent quietude.*

> You stiffnecked people, with uncircumcised hearts and ears! You are just like your fathers: you always resist the Holy Spirit! Was there ever a prophet your fathers did not persecute? They even killed those who predicted the coming of the righteous one. And now you have betrayed and murdered him—you who have received the law that was put into effect through angels but have not obeyed it. . . .
>
> When they heard this, they were furious and gnashed their teeth at him. . . . They covered their ears and yelling at the top of their voices, they all rushed at him, dragged him out of the city, and began to stone him.

Stephen's last remark, "You who have received the law that was put into effect through angels have not obeyed it," is most apropos of our own generation. What nation has received God's law and benefited more from it than the United States? Now this generation tramples on that law.

Another similarity to our own day lies in the reaction of his accusers when he answers them so well, so roundly, and so boldly, "When they heard this they were furious. . . . They covered their ears . . . yelling at the top of their voices." Certainly the media reactions to Christians who take a stand today are not much more than this. No real attempt is made at a reasoned reply.

Consider the vitriolic attack that those who despise the truth in our time will resort to. Pete Hamill, in an article entitled "TV Preachers Stoke the Hellfires," saw fit to lambast all those who preach the gospel on television on the basis of one psychotic man's tragic and horrible act. Hamill told his readers the story of Jimmy Doyle Meeks who, convinced that demons had taken possession of his two-and-a-half-year-old son and five-month-old daughter, tried to exorcise the demons by holding the children over a furnace grate. He killed his little daughter in this way and nearly did the same to his son. His defense attorney recognized the truth of the situation and planned on entering a plea of innocent by virtue of insanity. Hamill, instead of seeing this as the isolated act of a deranged man, found there were a number of connections to be made.

> But if Meeks is insane, he has plenty of company. All over America, at all hours of the day, the TV preachers are spewing their "Christian" messages about God and the devil to audiences full of people like Jimmy Doyle Meeks. The preachers are respected citizens; presidents take their calls; lesser politicians and network executives fear them; the tax laws make them rich. But they specialize in one thing—the peddling of fear. Fear of "secular humanism," communism, big government, labor unions, liberalism,

other Americans, all mixed up with fear of the Lord and fear of Satan.

We know their true enemies: reason, intelligence, pluralism.

If we make the proper syntactical connections in Hamill's article, we find that he has called the television preachers—all of them, without qualification—"insane." We find that he has presumed their audience largely so, since they are "full" of psychotic child-killers. (And Pete Hamill accuses *them* of "peddling fear.")[4] In the very worst instances of anti-Semitism we find writings filled with references to Jews as "child killers." Mr. Hamill, who obviously sets himself up as the defender of "reason, intelligence, pluralism," has adopted the same tactics. This is bigotry on an order that should revive faith in a literal devil in the most skeptical, modernist Christian! Who else could motivate such mouth-foaming blind hatred? Would Mr. Hamill similarly categorize all black civil rights leaders as villains because one deranged black man committed a rape which he explained as an act of black liberation?

As I've stated earlier, we Christians, when we accept the myth of neutrality, are often our own worst enemies. When we stir this kind of stinging criticism, these sharp-tongued, shrill rebukes from the reactionary incendiary secularist media, we are often surprised and hurt; we back off, wondering "what we have done wrong." But these occasions are the very times to press forward! Ours is not to be the defensive posture of cowering imbeciles. We should attack and defend ourselves on the basis of the contradictions inherent in the "liberal" bigotry we face.

The timidity of the Christian community must, in this desperate hour, be abandoned for the spirit of Peter and John and Stephen, and all the others in the New Testament who stood so firmly. The spirit of compromise with evil and death must be abandoned for the strength of pur-

pose found in Wilberforce, Shaftesbury, Luther, Bon-
hoeffer, and the others who have withstood the undermin-
ing of truth in their moment of history.

A frail little wisp of a woman, brown and wiry, with
bright sparrow eyes, Mother Theresa, was awarded the
Nobel Peace Prize. She was recognized and applauded by
the world in a way that would make many Christians feel,
"Well, they're not so bad, after all; look, they've recognized the work I've done." And these Christians would
soft-pedal or compromise what they had to say as a result.

Instead of accepting her award with the usual vapid
platitudes, Mother Theresa used that moment in the public
eye, to the surprise of the media, to make a ringing statement against abortion and the evils of an age that treats life
so cheaply. From her background of working with the
most destitute of the poor, she spoke of the unique preciousness of each human life, no matter how miserable it
may be, and against the evil of abortion. Because of her
personal involvement, her lifetime of work, her message
could not be gainsaid, and, because of the occasion, the
secularist media were forced to report her statements word
for word, without the usual sniveling wisecracks and
aspersions.

She used her moment in the sun to strike a blow for
truth, love, compassion, beauty, the dignity of each human being, the laws of Scriptures, and the love of God.
Her defiant stand condemns our silences—and the comfortable silence of so many Christian leaders and theologians.

It is time to ask a hard question, the question posed in
James. Are those who benefit from the warmth and "spirituality" of the Christian faith, and yet refuse to apply its
absolutes and truth and beauty to the world around them,
really Christians?

4 / The "Wall of Separation": the Myth of Neutrality in the Law and Politics

The Judeo-Christian influence on American society through the legal system and politics has declined to such an extent and so rapidly that we, as Christians, ought to be enraged. We find ourselves in a nation in which the law and indeed the so-called justice system is in such disarray as to be a mockery of the very words law and justice. Today, to put it bluntly, we find a nation that often frees its vicious criminals, and on the other hand, sanctions the murder of the *innocent* unborn. How has this come about? How and why has the much vaunted liberal voice, in fact, turned into the advocate of death as a cure to social ills? How is it that in the "land of the brave" there is more protection afforded by law to the snail darter and the sequoia than to the unborn human child?

To begin with, secularists have taken one phrase of Jefferson's in which he mentioned a "wall of separation" between church and state, and with it have, for their own ideological reasons, concocted an utterly ahistorical and unconstitutional doctrine of how church and state should relate to each other in American society. Our social institutions, through court edicts and authoritarian bureaucratic policy decisions, have been forced to expunge any vestige of the Judeo-Christian tradition which has, until recent years, been the ground on which the nation and indeed western civilization stood. In the guise of advocating "neutrality," secular humanists have replaced our nation's set of operating principles which derive from the Judeo-Christian tradition with another set of principles: these commit the United States to a materialistic view of truth, and have effectively established secular humanism as the only national religion.

Russ Pulliam,[1] one of the unhappily small number of outstanding journalists who are Christians, discussed the comical, yet tragic, blind alleys into which the secular conception of the separation of church and state has led us. In an editorial in the *Indianapolis News* on Saturday, December 19, 1981, Pulliam reviewed three stories involving free speech and the practice of religious liberty. The first took up an incident at DePaul University, where the student editors on the campus newspaper insisted upon running a story about a student who had been raped. The school tried to confiscate the paper, but then the administration thought about the students' right of free speech and rescinded their order. Next, at the *Daily Reveille* of Louisiana State University, officials censored an advertisement for contraceptives. "The ad, placed by a nearby drugstore, pictured two wine glasses and male contraceptives with the words: 'The perfect nightcap.' " The student editors found this restraint on their free speech "unacceptable." The last story came from Arizona State University where Christians were publishing their views about the bankruptcy of relativistic ethics and their dominance in the assumptions of many academic fields. There, "Rose Wertz, a sociology teacher, said she was planning to contact the ACLU for a possible lawsuit against the student newspaper. The potential crime: Violating church-state separation by publishing religious views in a state university newspaper." (So much for freedom of speech.) Pulliam comments:

That's the irony. Rape stories are all right—freedom

of the press. But a Christian world view violates the Constitution.

What is needed, beginning with the U.S. Supreme Court, is a new interpretation of the church-state clause, more consistent with what the Founding Fathers had in mind.

Because:

What's happened in recent years is that the Supreme Court and others have developed an odd interpretation [of the separation of church and state] that has little to do with the intent of the Constitution. Now we are told that all government institutions must be absolutely neutral toward religion and do absolutely nothing to advance it. That's an impossible task since all of life involves essentially religious issues.

What we are seeing today is that a great many "essentially religious issues" are being decided with no appeal to religious principle and, in fact, *a purposeful disregard of them.* The nightmare of the casual slaughter of the innocent in permissive abortion; the total breakdown of the family and sexual morality; the horrible use of medicine as a means of destroying life not only through abortion but also infanticide, deliberately removing treatment from unwanted handicapped children: these evils would not be possible, let alone "legal," in a culture in which Christians had as much power as the sheer numbers of us in our country should dictate. One can hardly believe the statistics of fifty million or so Americans who profess to be Bible-believing Christians. Nevertheless, even if only a fraction of that number had consistently stood up and voiced their opinions on these issues, they would have represented a massive political block. After all, the 1980 elections were decided by a margin of only a few million votes (44 million

Reagan, 35 million Carter, 6.5 million Anderson). Imagine the impact of just ten million swing votes in that framework.

The operating assumptions of the past did derive from the Judeo-Christian tradition. The roots of American constitutionalism, the concept of government limited by a system of checks and balances, grew out of Reformation Europe. Without knowing it at the time, two men laid the philosophical foundation for both the American Revolution and the Constitution which followed: Martin Luther and John Calvin. Like all the reformers, they stressed that the final authority in all matters was the Bible, God's Word and Law.

Later, following the ideas of Luther and other reformers, English theologian William Perkins wrote: "If it should fall out that men's laws be made of things evil, and forbidden by God, then there is no bond at all: but contrariwise, men are bound in conscience not to obey." In the Reformation tradition, God's law reigned supreme; while man was to "render unto Caesar what was Caesar's and unto God what was God's," those things which pertained to God, including the concepts of social justice and freedom found in the Bible, constituted the standards by which the laws of men might be judged. If those laws mandated wrongdoing, then the Christian ought to disobey those laws, in order to "obey God rather than man."

This was the view on which America was founded. On this basis, our forefathers committed acts of civil disobedience (e.g., throwing tea into Boston Harbor) because they saw certain statutes as unjust, in a fundamental sense contrary to the teaching of Scripture.[2]

The concept of "limited government under law" grew out of the Founders' understanding of history, which taught them that governments often contradicted and contravened the laws of God, particularly in regard to religious freedom. *Many among the Founders had fled the oppres-*

sive monarchies of Europe precisely because they were not given the religious freedom to worship as they pleased, and more importantly, to bring about social change in accordance with God's law. Far from intending to create a secular, let alone antireligious, state, the Founders wanted to create a society in which the work of the church, once unbound from governmental regulation, might in freedom flower in a variety of forms. They assumed that the Constitution, a distillation of Christian principles (life, liberty, etc.), would be interpreted in the light of the Judeo-Christian tradition, to which even the Deists and free-thinkers among them owed their conception of ethics.

Unfortunately, the activist and robust understanding of Christianity and the practice of Judeo-Christian truth held by the Founding Fathers grew weak and weak-kneed in later generations. Toward the end of the nineteenth century, a wave of pietism arose within the church, and the pietists looked away from their responsibilities in the world and cultivated "spiritual feelings." They mistook true spirituality for narcissism.

As a result, Christians increasingly withdrew from participating on the basis of their faith in political, legal, artistic, cultural, and educational matters—in fact, the Christian witness failed to address himself to *any* subject apart from conversion and life (if it can be called that) within the church. Pietism, then as now, made Christianity comfortable by making it unreal.[3]

In the vacuum created by the retreat of the church, inhuman and pagan ideas were revived. These were especially destructive in the areas of government, law, the arts, and politics.[4]

All of this paved the way to our own era where we find ourselves as an embattled Christian minority of *tiny proportions,* not numerically, but as far as any voice goes.

How many major national newspapers have an editorial slant from a Judeo-Christian perspective? How often do you see television films, specials, or shows that reflect or sympathetically discuss the Judeo-Christian view of life? What political party or organization has kept the promises it has made in its political platform, to the prolife community?[5]

A legal *coup d'etat* has occurred. The fundamental emphases of the framers have been subverted. The federal government is no longer denied those powers not specifically granted in the Constitution. The powers of the federal government and those of the courts are no longer deliberately few and defined, but *total* and *arbitrary*. In the humanistic conception of law, the citizen is the creature of the state; his rights are granted not by God, but by the state, and therefore the state can take them away if it likes. Law has truly become a matter of the survival of the fittest, the will of the strong and vocal over the weak and silent.

Because the fetus's scream cannot be heard in the gloom of the amniotic fluid, but the proabortionists can gather on the steps of the court and agitate, the proabortionists win the day! Truly the law of the jungle. Truly might makes right!

Many federal judges, including members of the Supreme Court, have extended the effects of this liberal humanistic legal revolution by usurping the powers of the legislature. Their "judicial activism," in substituting the anti-people premises of secular humanism for those of the Judeo-Christian tradition, has resulted in many decisions totally out of keeping with the traditions of our country. They have been so successful in imposing their novel ideology that *they* are now accepted as the status quo; judges who hold fast to our nation's traditions have become the exception and must now defend their "un-American" viewpoint.

In his book, *The Second American Revolution,* John Whitehead cites the Carter appointment of Patricia Wald to the United States Circuit Court of Appeals for Washington, D.C., as an example of how readily the most extreme of judicial activists are accepted. The facts about Patricia Wald take on particular significance since her court, because of its location, hands down many precedent-setting decisions.

Comparing the "institution of children" to the "institution of slavery," Patricia Wald wrote that children should be legally "independent" of their parents, and able to challenge them in court, thus placing the authority of the judge over the child and above his natural parents. Wald's philosophy, if implemented, would totally overturn the tradition of the family in the United States.[6]

During the confirmation hearings before the United States Senate for Wald's nomination, there was opposition to the appointment. Senator Gordon Humphrey stated, "The Wald nomination is a case which is outrageous. Here is a nominee who would radically alter the traditional family structure by virtually abolishing parental authority and who would empower a child to formally challenge his parents whenever, in the child's opinion, the parents were violating his civil rights." Naturally, Wald's appointment was not stopped by a weak-kneed and compromising Senate, and she was confirmed.

To understand the extent to which our society has been stolen from us by an inhuman elite, imagine a Christian stating his philosophy as clearly as Wald stated hers and being confirmed to sit on a major bench. Imagine the reaction to a nominee stating: "I am a Christian, and therefore, all my decisions shall be based on a traditional understanding of Judeo-Christian principles. Further, I shall take the traditional base of the common law of jurisprudence as my guide. I shall fight to overturn the liberal, humanistic decisions and precedents which have gone before (especially in the areas of the family and the public educational system). I shall fight for compassionate Judeo-Christian principles and absolutes as the law of the land." Do you think he or she would be confirmed? No! His secularist counterpart, however, can be appointed and state his philosophy *even more vehemently,* and as a "neutral" judge, be confirmed. Thus again, the double standard, the myth of neutrality, is in full force.

The Senate confirmation hearings of Sandra O'Connor's nomination to the Supreme Court reveal the in-built prejudices of the legal and political communities today. O'Connor, as a "strict constructionist" or one who opposes judicial activism, felt compelled to avow her "neutrality." Responding to Senator Strom Thurmond's question about her views on abortion, Judge O'Connor said:

> May I preface my response by saying that the personal view and philosophies, in my view, of a Supreme Court Justice and indeed any judge should be set aside insofar as it is possible to do that in resolving matters that come before the court.[7]

She went on to say that, while she personally is opposed to abortion as a means of birth control, she could not comment on *Roe v. Wade,* the decision by the Supreme Court in 1973 which struck down every state's law against abortion and effectively legalized it, not wanting to prejudge the issue, which might necessitate that she disqualify herself when the abortion issue came before the court again. Here again, the point is that traditionalists must affirm they can be "broad-minded," whereas a nominee like Wald can be as committed to her secularist perspective as she likes.

But simple neutrality on the part of Judge O'Connor was not enough for some senators. Convinced that "as a woman" O'Connor must share the judicial activist faith, Senator Biden gave Judge O'Connor the chance to agree with a professor of the University of Virginia Law School, that a Supreme Court nominee should be "a public person, one whose experience and outlook enables her to mediate between tradition and change . . . accommodating law for the change in need and perception." Senator Kennedy asked whether Judge O'Connor could agree with Justice Stevens' statement about the discretionary powers of judges, that "there are many, many cases in which affirmative remedies are found to be appropriate and would be sustained on appeal." In these instances and others, liberal senators were clearly begging O'Connor to reassure them that she was "one of us": someone who would compromise the principles of the Constitution in deference to public opinion, opinion that the liberal elite control; someone who would insure that society would become increasingly secular.

The greatest instance of liberal hypocrisy during the O'Connor hearings came about when prolife advocates, who were worried about O'Connor's past votes in the Arizona legislature, were told by Senator Metzenbaum that "I find something un-American about any particular candidate or any particular appointee being judged on the basis of one issue and one issue alone." One wonders why Senator Metzenbaum did not rally to Dr. Koop on similar grounds, since opposition to his appointment was on the sole ground of his favoring a prolife position (p. 288 of the O'Connor Hearings). In rebuttal, Senator East observed:

> If we had a nominee—which we have not had—but if we had a nominee who had a tainted record, let us say, on their attitude toward race, or if they had a tainted attitude on blacks or Jews or any other prominent group in the great American melting pot, that would be looked upon as deeply and profoundly suspect and perhaps infecting the whole, and it would not suffice to come in and say, "Yes, but they are rather strong on other things. . . ."

The unspoken pressures evident during these hearings, and those hypocritically absent in the case of a Patricia Wald, *show that the system now has a built-in bias against Judeo-Christian belief.* Traditionalists must "judge the case on its merits," while secularists can give free reign to their preconceptions and are encouraged to usurp the functions of the legislature through the exercise of their "discretionary" powers. *Christians cannot be "one issue" advocates, but their opponents can make any issue they feel strongly about decisive.* Of course racism should disqualify any nominee to the federal bench; equally, a proabortion position should be sufficient grounds for disqualification: those politicians who will not see the similarity of these human rights issues are simply pandering to a radically misguided part of their constituencies.

If anyone is still under the impression that the court system remains neutral about life and death decisions, consider these cases.

George F. Will, in a column headed 'The Killing Will Not Stop' wrote describing the case of "Baby Doe" who was starved to death by court permission in April 1982 in Indiana.

> The baby was born in Bloomington, Ind., the sort of academic community where medical facilities are more apt to be excellent than moral judgments are. Like one of every 700 or so babies, this one had Down's syndrome, a genetic defect involving varying degrees of retardation and, sometimes, serious physical defects.
> The baby needed serious but feasible surgery to enable food to reach its stomach. The parents refused the surgery, and presumably refused to yield custody to any of the couples eager to become the baby's guardians. The parents chose to starve their baby to death.
> Their lawyer concocted an Orwellian euphemism for this refusal of potentially life-saving treatment—"Treatment to do nothing." It is an old story: language must be

mutilated when a perfumed rationalization of an act is incompatible with a straightforward description of the act.

Indiana courts, accommodating the law to the *Zeitgeist,* refused to order surgery, and thus sanctioned the homicide. Common sense and common usage require use of the word "homicide." The law usually encompasses homicides by negligence. The Indiana killing was worse. It was the result of premeditated, aggressive, tenacious action, in the hospital and in courts.

Such homicides can no longer be considered aberrations, or culturally incongruous. They are part of a social program to serve the convenience of adults by authorizing adults to destroy inconvenient young life. The parents' legal arguments, conducted in private, reportedly emphasized—what else?—"freedom of choice." The freedom to choose to kill inconvenient life is being extended, precisely as predicted, beyond fetal life to categories of inconvenient infants, such as Down's syndrome babies. There is no reason—none—to doubt that if the baby had not had Down's syndrome the operation would have been ordered without hesitation, almost certainly, by the parents or, if not by them, by the courts. Therefore the baby was killed because it was retarded. I defy the parents and their medical and legal accomplices to explain why, by the principles affirmed in this case, parents do not have a right to kill by calculated neglect any Down's syndrome child—regardless of any medical need—or any other baby that parents decide would be inconvenient.

Indeed, the parents' lawyer implied as much when, justifying the starvation, he emphasized that even if successful the surgery would not have corrected the retardation. That is, the Down's syndrome was sufficient reason for starving the baby. But the broader message of this case is that being an unwanted baby is a capital offense.

In 1973 the Supreme Court created a virtually unrestrictable right to kill fetuses. Critics of the ruling were alarmed because the court failed to dispatch the burden of saying why the fetus, which unquestionably is alive, is not protectable life. Critics were alarmed also because the court, having incoherently emphasized "viability," offered no intelligible, let alone serious, reason why birth should be the point at which discretionary killing stops. Critics feared what the Indiana homicide demonstrates: the killing will not stop.

The values and passions, as well as the logic of some portions of the "abortion rights" movement, have always pointed beyond abortion, toward something like the Indiana outcome, which affirms a broader right to kill. Some people have used the silly argument that it is impossible to know when life begins. (The serious argument is about when a "person" protectable by law should be said to exist.) So what could be done about the awkward fact that a newborn, even a retarded newborn, is so incontestably alive?

The trick is to argue that the lives of certain kinds of newborns, like the lives of fetuses, are not sufficiently "meaningful"—a word that figured in the 1973 ruling—to merit any protection that inconveniences an adult's freedom of choice.

The Indiana parents consulted with doctors about the "treatment" they chose. But this was not at any point, in any sense, a medical decision. Such homicides in hospitals are common and will become more so now that a state's courts have given them an imprimatur. There should be interesting litigation now that Indiana courts—whether they understand this or not—are going to decide which categories of newborns (besides Down's syndrome children) can be killed by mandatory neglect.

Hours after the baby died, the parents' lawyer was on the "CBS Morning News" praising his clients' "courage." He said, "The easiest thing would have been to defer, let somebody else make that decision." Oh? Someone had to deliberate about whether or not to starve the baby? When did it become natural, even necessary, in Indiana for parents to sit around debating whether to love or starve their newborns?

The lawyer said it was a "no-win situation" because "there would have been horrific trauma—trauma to the child who would never have enjoyed a—a quality of life of—of any sort, trauma to the family, trauma to society."

In this "no-win" situation, the parents won: the county was prevented from ordering surgery; prospective adopters were frustrated; the baby is dead. Furthermore, how is society traumatized whenever a Down's syndrome baby is not killed? It was, I believe George Orwell who warned that insincerity is the enemy of sensible language.

Someone should counsel the counselor to stop babbling about Down's syndrome children not having "any sort" of quality of life. The task of convincing communities to provide services and human sympathy for the retarded is difficult enough without incoherent lawyers laying down the law about whose life does and whose does not have "meaning."

The *Washington Post* headlined its report: "The Demise of 'Infant Doe' " (the name used in court). "Demise," indeed. That suggests an event unplanned, even perhaps unexplained. ("The Demise of Abraham Lincoln?") The *Post's* story began:

"An Indiana couple, backed by the state's highest court and the family doctor, allowed their severely retarded newborn baby to die last Thursday night. . . ."

But "severely retarded" is a misjudgment (also appearing in the *New York Times*) that is both a cause and an effect of cases like the one in Indiana. There is no way of knowing, and no reason to believe, that the baby would have been "severely retarded." A small fraction of Down's syndrome children are severely retarded. The degree of retardation cannot be known at birth. Furthermore, such children are dramatically responsive to infant stimulation and other early interventions. But, like other children, they need to eat.

When a commentator has a direct personal interest in an issue, it behooves him to say so. Some of my best friends are Down's syndrome citizens. (Citizens is what Down's syndrome children are if they avoid being homicide victims in hospitals.)

Jonathan Will, 10, fourth-grader and Orioles fan (and the best Wiffle-ball hitter in southern Maryland), has Down's syndrome. He does not "suffer from" (as newspapers are wont to say) Down's syndrome. He suffers from nothing, except anxiety about the Orioles' lousy start.

He is doing nicely, thank you. But he is bound to have quite enough problems dealing with society—receiving rights, let alone empathy. He can do without people like Infant Doe's parents, and courts like Indiana's asserting by their actions the principle that people like him are less than fully human. On the evidence, Down's syndrome citizens have little to learn about being human from the people responsible for the death of Infant Doe.

Cases such as this are becoming common to the point of banality (like all great evils) in the United States today. This particular case received more than usual public attention. The State Supreme Court of Indiana clearly chose on the basis of the present humanistic and selfish consensus to uphold the "rights" of the parents over that of the life of the child.

The Oklahoma Supreme Court ruled in September 1981 that a twelve-year-old girl who had become pregnant should be "entitled" to an abortion *over her mother's religious objections.* The mother (a member of the Church of Holiness) had asked the court to uphold her contention that she should make the decision because her daughter was too young to decide for herself. Nevertheless, the court ruled the girl "a deprived child" and ordered her to be made a ward of the state so that her "pregnancy could be terminated." Additionally, the court even ordered the mother not to talk to her daughter about the abortion![8]

In 1980 the California Supreme Court declared that the parents of Phillip Becker, a retarded child, should not be forced by doctors, who were concerned for the child's well-being, to let the boy have an operation that would correct a heart defect, prolong the child's life, and make it more comfortable. Although social workers, doctors, and friends of the child all affirmed in sworn testimony that the boy was capable of learning and enjoying a full life, his parents, in the guise of "compassion for the boy," refused to allow the operation. The "compassion" of the parents was highly suspect, since the boy had been institutionalized and his parents almost never visited him. *And yet the court ruled against the boy, condemning him to an early and painful death.*[9]

An exception to these deadly decisions serves to point out the incredible insensitivity of those caught up in the myth of neutrality. In late October, 1981, a judge in Kalamazoo, Michigan, had a case come before him in which he was ordered by a federal judge to decide on whether a twelve-year-old girl should be *forced* to have an abortion *against her own will and her mother's will.* Fortunately, this judge, a compassionate man, decided that the girl could keep her baby; he noted, in his ruling, that this was the girl's will in the matter and that the girl's family concurred and looked forward to receiving the baby into its home.

Nevertheless, the proabortion forces, who style themselves "child advocates," (with friends like these, who needs enemies?!?), called for this judge's removal from the bench *for not forcing the girl to have an abortion.* They insisted that the judge was "biased"; *in other words, they would have preferred a judge who took a proabortion position.* All of this, despite the fact that the girl was six months pregnant at the time *and the baby could survive outside the mother's womb!* The abortion advocates, these "child advocates," would have killed a child who, even by the pagan permissive standards of the Supreme Court ruling, should have been protected by law![10] This case shows the limits to which proabortion advocates are willing to go; arguing on the basis of extreme cases out of "kindness" for pregnant women, their values are in reality simply an extrapolation of what *they* would choose; to present them with a young girl who has the courage to love and sacrifice for a young infant disturbs their ideas about what they require of themselves, and so they tried to suppress this good example, making a mockery of their professed belief in "choice."

The first three cases and the reaction of the proabortion forces to the fourth demonstrate that "neutrality" in such cases simply cannot exist. Either a child is killed or not killed. The courts, in contrast to their views on capital punishment, all too often think that death is the preferable solution, and, like the firing squad in its thousandth execution, maintain a callous boredom towards life. When the humanist cannot cure, he is apparently all too eager to kill.

The companion magazine to the PBS television series *Hard Choices* contains an article written by the narrator of the series, Gerald Dworkin; in this piece he spells out the humanist's social engineering rationale: "Can its own death ever be considered a good thing for the fetus? I would argue that at the least, the notion makes sense—that under some circumstances the fetus is better off dead—and that in some cases it is true." (Copyright © 1980, KCTS/9, The Regents of the University of Washington, p. 7.)

So it is that the courts will remove a minor from her parents to help her kill her baby, but will not remove a child from his parents to save his life! This can hardly be described as impartiality, let alone benevolence!

The increasingly cruel humanistic perspective of the courts has, of course, influenced decisions in many other areas. The extirpation of any expression of public belief in God ranks second to abortion as the most devastating result of this viewpoint.

To combat the increasing chaos in society, especially in education and student behavior, Kentucky sought to bring the humane and civilizing realization to its young citizens that, in fact, there were laws and guiding principles upon which life could be founded. They required, in 1978, that the Ten Commandments, the very basis of western civilization's laws, be posted in the public school classrooms of that state. Predictably, however, in 1980 the

Supreme Court struck down this wise decision, ruling that the law violated the First Amendment's prohibition against "establishing a religion." This must seem to anybody an interpretation of the amendment that bends over backwards to placate the antireligious sectors in our society, at the expense not only of truth, but just plain common sense as well. But this is only in keeping with the Supreme Court's prior ruling that children may recite the pledge of allegiance with its "one nation under God" phrase only because, in the court's mind, the children are not affirming something true but only alluding to a historical misconception. It's gone that far.

We can expect more decisions in the future which will not only purge the nation of its historical religious affirmations, but which will narrow and circumscribe the sphere in which religious affirmations may be made. In a decision that will likely be a harbinger of things to come, the Supreme Court recently refused to hear a case, *Brandon* v. *Board of Education*, in which high school students sought the right to use a classroom after school for a religious meeting. The Court's deaf ear left standing a lower court's ruling that the students were violating the Constitution. The Supreme Court, in footnote 13 to an earlier case, *Widmar* v. *Vincent*, which allowed university students the right to meet in the facilities of their public university, stated: "This case is different from cases in which religious groups claim that the denial of facilities *not* available to other groups deprives them of their rights under the Free Exercise Clause."[11]

The *Catholic League Newsletter*, commenting on *Brandon*, said that this was totally in error, that the facilities the high school students wanted to use were available to other student groups and even the general public. In addition, the Court in its footnote to *Widmar* claimed that such cases as *Brandon* were being argued on the basis of the freedom of religion when, in fact, *Brandon* was argued on the grounds of free speech, as was the successful *Widmar* case. In the absence of cogent reasons to the contrary, the Court left us to draw the conclusion that high school students meeting after hours at their school for religious instruction and prayer must be unconstitutional because, unlike university students, younger students can be influenced by what they hear. Free speech, it seems, is fine as long as no one runs the "risk" of conversion.

Does anyone seriously think that if the Founding Fathers came back and looked at all of this they would side with the secularist revision of history, which might be summarized: "America was always a pluralistic secularist state which may have tolerated a few religious people but never gave them any real part in society"? Can you imagine them approving the Court's decision that it is unconstitutional to post the Ten Commandments? That it is unconstitutional for high school students to meet together in a classroom to pray? That a convicted murderer-rapist have excessive protection under the law, while the very *personhood* and right to live be denied 25 percent of *all* babies conceived? That a child be starved to death because he has Down's syndrome?

The courts, these paragons of "pluralism" and "open-mindedness," have in effect said, "You don't need God: the nation has never been 'under God': but don't worry; after all, you have us."

Increasingly, it seems, the courts' decisions come down on the bigoted, secularist side. In effect they are saying, "Everything goes except religious principle."

We have traded religious absolutes of life and compassion for the secularist absolutes of economic expediency and death. We have traded religious teachers for secularist prophets, the wisdom of the Apostle Paul for the evangelistic pop-science crusades of the likes of a Carl Sagan and his *Cosmos*. We have replaced the Law given to Moses with the whims of naive, faltering humans.

It is time for a massive assault on this humanistic and bigoted culture in the name of freedom and compassion. Christians should be *shamed* by the zealous activity of the liberal elite whose houses are built on sand, while we, with our houses supposedly built on the rock, sit silently and look on. The ACLU aggressively files approximately six thousand left-wing, often antireligious activist cases a year. The passive Christian Legal Society is just now taking its first steps toward countering the proponents of secularism. Planned Parenthood never rests in their effort to have more abortions performed. The Christian Medical Association has, in the main, avoided the issue of abortion as "divisive." All too often the Christian response has been limited to another conference, while the secularist elite is actively engaged in *real events.* Using politics and what's left of the law, we must stall the advance of secularism and then, in the name of liberty, regain the ground we have lost. Our insane society must be put right once again. The innocent must be protected, the sanctity of each life upheld. If it takes one or fifty years, compassionate Judeo-Christian truth *must be reestablished.*

Common sense must be restored and true moral values upheld. The lunatic liberal experiment with human lives must be seen as the horrible failure it is and be abandoned. However they try to deceive us, whatever forms their schizophrenic claims take, we must persevere. We must subvert the secularist, antireligious bigots in their attempt to impose on us, by force of law, a disgustingly ugly society.

Where have we been? Where are we going? What must we do? These questions must be uppermost in the minds of Christians if we wish not only to survive this century intact, but also to practice the compassion that is commanded in Scripture. We must realize that there is no compassion in conveniently passing by on the other side of the road from those who are in distress; we must take the parable of the Good Samaritan seriously enough to *apply it* to individuals, to unborn children, to the "Baby Does" of this nation. Non-involvement is not something that can be justified biblically: we *are* our brother's keeper.

We must *vote*. We must hold those we *elect* to the promises they make. We must *agitate* for life and compassion. We must *undermine* the lies and bigotry of the liberal, humanistic elite. We must *organize* ourselves to speak with unanimity on the key issues of the right to *life* and *freedom* to express ourselves in *every* area of concern. We must stand for the *freedom* to educate our children *without interference from the pagan government that now rules us*. We must insure that the church has the freedom to effect change in society. We must resist and be willing to disobey the inhuman, excessive whimsy of our courts. We must act in compassion for the murdered children, the broken individuals from shattered homes, this whole sad, shepherdless generation. We must *actively* resist and challenge the arrogant courts, judges, doctors, and officials who would stand in the place of God. We must reestablish the beauty and fullness in love of a Christian nation that was once ours. Mercy and justice can—must, if need be—be made to kiss each other again.

5 / The Collapse of Moral, Cultural, and Sexual Attitudes: the Failure of Humanistic Double-think

Abortion, it was argued, way back when, was to relieve the suffering of thirteen-year-old girls who had been raped and mothers who would die if they bore children. (Abortions had been given in this last context, anyway.)

Only a decade later we find a reality of one million five hundred thousand permissive abortions a year. Only a tiny fraction of these abortions bear any resemblance to the emotionally shrill cases (life of the mother, incest, rape) on which the whole landslide of killing was argued into legality. An admission that things have turned out slightly differently than envisioned? Never.

There is a myth of neutrality and a deceit in the attitudes toward sexual, cultural, and moral issues today which boggles the mind. Any excuse is used as a wedge to open the door for some new Utopian inhumanity like abortion. Then when the door is open, all the original arguments are forgotten, and the taking of innocent life becomes as commonplace as soda pop.

In the companion magazine for the prodeath television series *Hard Choices,* William B. Provine introduces the topic of eugenics, which is "the science of improving human beings through breeding." He reviews the history of eugenics, how its "ideals" were used to justify the slaughter of six million Jews and the sterilization of two hundred thousand other people.[1] Provine notes that eugenics practically disappeared after World War II because nobody wanted "to be associated with the Nazi atrocities." But in Mr. Provine's mind no such association seems to bother him, and eugenics should now be resurrected:

> Eugenics has not disappeared, and the situation has changed. Eugenics is now based on better science and more sophisticated concepts than in the past. Some applications of eugenics are becoming standard practice, and we can expect its use to expand if, as predicted, the world's resources become ever scarcer. The new eugenics will force some very difficult choices between individual freedom and public welfare, and, as I argue elsewhere, we have to look to ourselves as human beings to write the moral rules that will govern these choices [p. 9].

This will be one of the most flagrant current examples of science cut off from any moral imperative, in all of its neo-fascist horror. The "better science" and "more sophisticated concepts" to which Mr. Provine alludes are the recent discoveries about DNA, about *how* genetics works, and about how we can manipulate genetic information. The moral question, the question of *why*, has not changed *in any way* since the end of World War II. If we can abort babies—the "standard practice" to which he refers—with greater skill, and if we are beginning to make the discoveries which will give us the power to make human beings to order, that does not change the question of whether we *ought* to do these things. Hitler had poisonous gas at his disposal, a relatively painless and certainly more efficient means of mass murder than was at the disposal of other despots. Does this in any way make Hitler's actions less evil? Certainly not. Mr. Provine, an "ethicist," totally begs the ethical question. He also employs the scare tactic of making us feel that, in a world of ever more scarce resources (a highly debatable point in itself),[2] it may well come down to a choice between genetic engineering and our own lives, "resources" having replaced the "Jewish

plot" of the earlier eugenics. Someone like Provine elimi-
nates the possibility of Judeo-Christian ethics, reserves the
voodoo-mumbo-jumbo "knowledge" of science for a
chosen few, and effectively puts us in the hands of the high
priests of technology like himself, with no recourse but to
submit happily to the inevitable. His would be a world in
which the social engineers and the judiciary arbiters of
"rights" would have the individual at their mercy. Mr.
Provine has perhaps read *Brave New World* and mistaken it
for a travel brochure to a country to which he would
apparently like to go and to which we will be forced to
accompany him.

This is not a new phenomenon for the idealistic, Utopian liberal humanist whose memory is always conveniently short. Eugenics has been tried and the result was
the holocaust. Rousseau and Voltaire argued for sexual
liberation, a return to nature, and a breaking of the bonds
of "religious restriction"—which Voltaire called "the infamy"—to free man and prepare him for existence in the
humanistic Utopia. That was the theory. The fact, the
actual outworking in history? Bloody tyranny, forty
thousand peasants guillotined; and after the reign of terror
ended, France submitted to the total dictatorship of Napo-
leon. The utopian, religion-free society of the Soviet
Union was to have been a "workers' paradise." The reality
half a century later? Grinding misery, total oppression,
and not even the minimum material benefits taken for
granted in the West. Abortion was to alleviate a few
hardship cases but has become a casual, silent holocaust.

But still the world does not draw the obvious conclusions: that we must abandon this brutal anti-God, liberal,
humanistic philosophy and never let it show its head
again. But no. Press on, no matter what the cost. Just as
abortion followed permissive sex, like day follows night,
so now eugenics is to follow abortion. Infanticide already
is in our midst.

The *Village Voice,* a newspaper published in New York, is not exactly known as a bastion of conservative thinking; in fact, whenever they publish anything that could, by any stretch of the imagination, be labeled "moderate" or "right of center," it appears under their column, "Other Voices"—their nod to "objectivity." Remember, abortion was going to help teenage rape and incest victims; the following article by a proabortion advocate spells out what the reality of the matter has turned out to be.

The article was headed, "Abortion Chic—The Attraction of Wanted-Unwanted Pregnancies" by Leslie Savan, *Village Voice,* February 4, 1981. In this article the author first discusses how abortion has become "subliminally chic" in feminist circles and how many women are "replacing having children with having abortions." She then quotes a study by Kristin Luker which found that only 6 percent of 500 women who had received abortions had been regularly using birth control when they conceived. It now appears, according to the author, that many women are becoming pregnant *without any intention of carrying the baby to term.* This, of course, is just one of the tragic consequences of the easy availability of abortion.

But *why* are more and more women getting pregnant with the express intention of aborting? Here are the reasons Leslie Savan gives:

> • A desire to know if we're fertile, especially if we've postponed pregnancy until later in life (waiting for that perfect career/relationship ratio). I have several friends who say they've intentionally done this. But idle curiosity was not always the reason. Two-thirds of the women in Luker's study said a doctor has told them they couldn't get pregnant (when in fact the message was probably something less final like, "Your tilted uterus could make conception difficult"). Infrequent but hardly unheard-of side effects of abortion, such as subsequent miscarriage or sterility due to tubal infection—not to mention recurrent

pain—make it a terrible irony for women who got pregnant only to see if they could.

● To test the commitment of the man. Will he marry me, or at least put up half the money for the operation? Presumably this tactic was made obsolete by the women's movement, but it still goes on, though most people are unaware of it. Men who tacitly encourage women to forget contraception on occasion also enjoy the thrills of this risk.

● Abortion as a rite of passage, somewhere after first menses and (usually) before childbirth. Not all women take part in it, as not all go to the prom, but the fact that more women are aborting makes it more permissible, even intriguing. A friend of mine couldn't get it out of her mind how a woman she knew got pregnant and aborted to test her fertility. It went so neatly. A year later, my friend didn't use her diaphragm, figuring her period was due soon and anyway, if she did get pregnant, she'd at least find out if at the late age of 26 she could conceive. She did and loved the week she knew she was pregnant. She aborted and felt part of a club.

● Abortion as a kind of childbirth. Like delivery, it ends a pregnancy, it puts us "in touch with our bodies," and it stirs our maternal feelings, if only by regret. Rites without responsibility.

● As a desirable tinge of tragedy. "I've been through a lot. I've had an abortion." It provides a "real-life experience" and seems to increase our participation in the great themes of life and death.

● As a way of eating our cake and having it too. Torn between "femininity" and feminism, getting pregnant "proves" we are feminine while getting an abortion "proves" we are feminist.

After giving us this incredible laundry list of delusion, narcissism, and irresponsibility, the author voices a few qualms about what the behavior of her sister proabortionists might signify. Have they considered, for example, that their actions perhaps indicate a lack of "seriousness" on their part (whatever that means)? That they might have indulged in sloganeering? That they may be guilty of lacking imagination? The author brings up these strange misgivings with the forlorn hope of trying to inject a note of morality into the proabortion position.

But what about the real issues in the abortion controversy, such as: is the fetus a human being or not? The author conveniently doesn't know. Then what about the idea that it is barbaric for humans to kill their own offspring, something even dumb animals and savages know better than to do? That is not even discussed.

As abortion becomes more and more a part of American life, the number of people committed to it by direct association grows. Those who have supported it in the past want to see it continue as a sign that their opinions and actions were justified. And the medical profession and those associated with it stand to lose a great amount of easy profit. Greed, arrogance, and *guilt* have become a powerful political force.

Nothing else but greed—and an orthodox understanding of evil and the censorship of the biased media—can explain why the facts in an article titled "Abortion," by Liz Jeffries and Rick Edmonds, published in the *Philadelphia Inquirer,* August 2, 1981, have not been widely circulated and publicized. It is quite a long article and cannot be quoted in full here. But I have excerpted a good part of it, and the entire article is included as an appendix. I strongly urge you to read all of it because it shows, without being alarmist or overly dramatic (indeed, the authors appear to be in favor of abortion themselves), the utter horror of abortion and how insensitive, corrupt, and willfully blind we have become.

A woman's scream broke the late-night quiet and brought two young obstetrical nurses rushing to Room 4456 of the University of Nebraska Medical Center. The patient, admitted for an abortion, had been injected 30 hours earlier with a salt solution, which normally kills the fetus and causes the patient to deliver a mass of lifeless tissue, in a process similar to a miscarriage.

This time, though, something had gone wrong. When nurse Marilyn Wilson flicked on the lights and pulled back the covers, she found, instead of the stillborn fetus she'd expected, a live 2½-pound baby boy, crying and moving his arms and legs there on the bed.

Dismayed, the second nurse, Joanie Fuchs, gathered the squirming infant in loose bedcovers, dashed down the corridor and called to the other nurses for help. She did not take the baby to an intensive care nursery, but deposited it instead on the stainless steel drainboard of a sink in the maternity unit's Dirty Utility Room—a large closet where bedpans are emptied and dirty linens stored. Other nurses and a resident doctor gathered and gaped.

Finally, a head nurse telephoned the patient's physician, Dr. C. J. LaBenz, at home, apparently waking him.

"He told me to leave it where it was," the head nurse testified later, "just to watch it for a few minutes, that it would probably die in a few minutes."

This was in Omaha, in September 1979. It was nothing new. Hundreds of times a year in the United States, an aborted fetus emerges from the womb kicking and alive. Some survive. A baby girl in Florica, rescued by nurses who found her lying in a bedpan, is 5 years old now and doing well. Most die. The Omaha baby lasted barely 2½ hours after he was put in the closet with the dirty linen.

Always, their arrival is met with shock, dismay and confusion.

When such a baby is allowed to die and the incident becomes known, the authorities often try to prosecute the doctor. This has happened several dozen times in the past eight years, most recently in the case of Dr. LaBenz, who is to go on trial in Omaha this fall on two counts of criminal abortion. But interviews with nurses, some of them visibly anguished, uncovered dozens of similar cases that never reached public attention.

In fact, for every case that does become known, a

hundred probably go unreported. Dr. Willard Cates, an expert on medical statistics who is chief of abortion surveillance for the Center for Disease Control in Atlanta, estimates that 400 to 500 abortion live births occur every year in the United States. That is only a tiny fraction of the nation's 1.5 million annual abortions. Still, it means that these unintended live births are literally an everyday occurrence.

They are little known because organized medicine, from fear of public clamor and legal action, treats them more as an embarrassment to be hushed up than a problem to be solved. "It's like turning yourself in to the IRS for an audit," Cates said. "What is there to gain? The tendency is not to report because there are only negative incentives. . . ."

By ignoring the problem of abortion live births, the courts and the medical establishment are choosing to overlook a long, well-documented history of cases:

January 1969. Stobhill Hospital, Glasgow, Scotland: A custodian heard a cry from a paper bag in the snow beside an incinerator. He found a live baby. It was taken inside and cared for in the hospital's operating theater but died nine hours later. The infant's gestational age had been estimated at 26 weeks by the physician performing the abortion. It was actually closer to 32 weeks. No efforts were made to check for signs of life before the aborted baby was discarded. No charges were filed. Because the case had been written about in British medical journals, it was a matter of record—before abortion was legalized in this country—that such things could happen.

April 1973. Greater Bakersfield Hospital, Bakersfield, Calif.: A 4½-pound infant was born live following a saline abortion (induced by an injection of salt solution) performed by Dr. Xavier Hall Ramirez. Informed by phone, Dr. Ramirez ordered two nurses to discontinue administering oxygen to the baby. His instructions were countermandated by another doctor; the baby survived and later was placed for adoption. Ramirez was indicted for solicitation to commit murder. His attorney argued that a medical order based on medical opinion, no matter how mistaken, is privileged. Dr. Irvin M. Cushner of the University of California at Los Angeles, later to become a top health policy official in the Carter administration, testified that it was normal for Ramirez to expect the delivery of a dead or certain-to-die infant as the result of a saline abortion.

July 1974. West Penn Hospital, Pittsburgh: Dr. Leonard Laufe performed an abortion on a woman who contended she had been raped—though that and her account of when she became pregnant were later disputed. She had been turned down for an abortion at another hospital, where the term of her pregnancy was estimated at 26 to 31 weeks. Laufe put it at 20 to 22. The abortion, induced by an injection of prostaglandin, a substance that stimulates muscle contraction and delivery of the fetus, was filmed for use as an instructional film. The film showed the three-pound infant moving and gasping. Also, a nurse and a medical student testified that they had noticed signs of life. No charges were filed, however, after a coroner's inquest at which Laufe testified that the infant sustained fatal damage during delivery.

February 1975. Boston: Dr. Kenneth Edelin was convicted of manslaughter for neglecting to give care to a 24-week infant after a 1973 abortion at Boston City Hospital. Witnesses said Edelin held the infant down, constricting the flow of oxygen through the umbilical cord and smothering it. He was the first and only American doctor ever convicted on charges of failing to care for an infant born during an abortion. The conviction was overturned by the Massachusetts Supreme Court on the ground that improper instructions had been given to the jury. Edelin and his lawyer argued that he had taken no steps to care for the infant because it was never alive outside the womb.

March 1977. Westminster Community Hospital, Westminster, Calif.: A seven-month baby girl was born live after a saline abortion performed by Dr. William Waddill. A nurse testified that Waddill, when he got to the hospital, interrupted her efforts to help the baby's breathing. A fellow physician testified that he had seen Waddill choke the infant. "I saw him put his hand on this baby's neck and push down," said Dr. Ronald Cornelson. "He said, 'I can't find the goddamn trachea,' and 'This baby won't stop breathing.' " Two juries, finding Cornelson an emotional and unconvincing witness, deadlocked in two separate trials. Charges against Waddill were then dismissed. He had contended the infant was dying of natural causes by the time he got to the hospital.

July 1979. Cedars-Sinai Medical Center, Los Angeles: Dr. Boyd Cooper delivered an apparently stillborn infant, after having ended a problem pregnancy of 23 weeks. Half an hour later the baby made gasping attempts to breathe, but no efforts were made to resuscitate it because of its size (1 pound 2 ounces) and the wishes of the parents. The baby was taken to a small utility room that was used, among other things, as an infant morgue. Told of the continued gasping, Cooper instructed a nurse, "Leave the baby there—it will die." Twelve hours later, according to testimony of the nurse, Laura VanArsdale, she returned to work and found the infant still in the closet, still gasping.

Cooper then agreed to have the baby boy transferred to an intensive care unit, where he died four days later. A coroner's jury ruled the death "accidental" rather than natural but found nothing in Cooper's conduct to warrant criminal action.

A common thread in all these incidents is that life was recognized and the episode brought to light by someone other than the doctor. Indeed, there is evidence that doctors tend to ignore all but the most obvious signs of life in an abortion baby.

In the November 1974 newsletter of the International Correspondence Society of Obstetricians and Gynecologists, several doctors addressed a question from a practitioner who had written in an earlier issue that he was troubled by what to do when an aborted infant showed signs of life.

One was Dr. Ronald Bolognese, an obstetrician at Pennsylvania Hospital in Philadelphia, who replied:

"At the time of delivery, it has been our policy to wrap the fetus in a towel. The fetus is then moved to another room while our attention is turned to the care of [the woman]. She is examined to determine whether complete placental expulsion has occurred and the extent of vaginal bleeding. Once we are sure that her condition is stable, the fetus is evaluated. Almost invariably all signs of life have ceased."

(Bolognese recanted that statement in a 1979 interview. "That's not what we do now," he said. "We would transport it to the intensive care nursery.")

In addition, Dr. William Brenner of the University of North Carolina Medical School suggested that if breathing and movement persist for several minutes, "the patient's physician, if he is not in attendance, should probably be contacted and informed of the situation. The pediatrician on call should probably be apprised of the situation if signs of life continue."

Dr. Warren Pearse, executive director of the American College of Obstetrics and Gynecology, was asked in a 1979 interview what doctors do, as standard practice, to check whether an aborted fetus is alive.

"What you would do next [after expulsion] is nothing," Pearse said. "You assume the infant is dead unless it shows signs of life. You're dealing with a dead fetus unless there is sustained cardiac action or sustained respiration—it's not enough if there's a single heartbeat or an occasional gasp."

These seemingly callous policies are based on the assumption that abortion babies are too small or too damaged by the abortion process to survive and live meaningful lives. That is not necessarily the case, though, even for babies set aside and neglected in the minutes after delivery. . . .

. . . Nursing staffs have led a number of quiet revolts against late abortions. Two major hospitals in the Fort Lauderdale areas, for instance, stopped offering abortions in the late 1970s after protests from nurses who felt uncomfortable handling the lifelike fetuses.

A Grand Rapids, Mich., hospital stopped late-term abortions in 1977 after nurses made good on their threat not to handle the fetuses. One night they left a stillborn fetus lying in its mother's bed for an hour and a half, despite angry calls from the attending physician, who finally went in and removed it himself.

In addition, a number of hospital administrators have reported problems in mixing maternity and abortion patients—the latter must listen to the cries of newborn infants while waiting for the abortion to work. And it has proved difficult in general hospitals to provide round-the-clock staffing of obstetrical nurses willing to assist with the procedure.

One young nurse in the Midwest, who quit to go into teaching, remembers "a happy group of nurses" turning nasty to each other and the physicians because of conflicts over abortion. One day, she recalled, a woman physician "walked out of the operating room after doing six abortions. She smeared her hand [which was covered with blood] on mine and said, 'Go wash it off. That's the hand that did it.' "

Several studies have documented the distress that late abortion causes many nurses. Dr. Warren M. Hern, chief physician, and Billie Corrigan, head nurse, of the Boulder (Colo.) Abortion Clinic, presented a paper to a 1978 Planned Parenthood convention entitled "What About Us? Staff Reactions . . ."

The clinic, one of the largest in the Rocky Mountain states, specializes in the D&E (dilation and evacuation) method of second-trimester abortions, a procedure in which the fetus is cut from the womb in pieces. Hern and Corrigan reported that eight of the 15 staff members surveyed reported emotional problems. Two said they worried about the physician's psychological well-being. Two reported horrifying dreams about fetuses, one of which involved the hiding of fetal parts so that other people would not see them.

"We have produced an unusual dilemma," Hern and Corrigan concluded. "A procedure is rapidly becoming recognized as the procedure of choice in late abortion, but those capable of performing or assisting with the procedure are having strong personal reservations about participating in an operation which they view as destructive and violent."

Dr. Julius Butler, a professor of obstetrics and gynecology at the University of Minnesota Medical School, is concerned about studies suggesting that D&E is the safest method and should be used more widely. "Remember," he said, "there is a human being at the other end of the table taking that kid apart.

"We've had guys drinking too much, taking drugs, even a suicide or two. There have been no studies I know of of the problem, but the unwritten kind of statistics we see are alarming."

"You are doing a destructive process," said Dr. William Benbow Thompson of the University of California at Irvine. "Arms, legs, chests come out in the forceps. It's not a sight for everybody."

Not all doctors think the stressfulness is overwhelming. The procedure "is a little bit unpleasant for the physician," concludes Dr. Mildred Hanson, a petite woman in her early 50s who does eight to 10 abortions a day in a clinic in Minneapolis, just a few miles across town from where Butler works. "It's easier to . . . leave someone else—namely a nurse—to be with the patient and do the dirty work.

"There is a lot in medicine that is unpleasant" but necessary—like amputating a leg—she argues, and doctors shouldn't let their own squeamishness deprive patients of a procedure that's cheaper and less traumatic.

However, Dr. Nancy Kaltreider, an academic psychiatrist at the University of San Francisco, has found in several studies "an unexpectedly strong reaction" by the assisting staff to late-abortion procedures. For nurses, she hypothesizes, handling tissues that resemble a fully formed baby "runs directly against the medical emphasis on preserving life."

The psychological wear-and-tear from doing late abortions is obvious. Philadelphia's Dr. Bolognese, who seven years ago was recommending wrapping abortion live-borns in a towel, has stopped doing late abortions.

"You get burned out," he said. Noting that his main research interest is in the management of complicated obstetrical cases, he observed: "It seemed kind of schizophrenic, to be doing that on the one hand [helping women with problem pregnancies to have babies] and do abortions."

Dr. John Franklin, medical director of Planned Parenthood of Southeastern Pennsylvania, was the plaintiff in a 1979 Supreme Court case liberalizing the limits on late abortions. He does not do such procedures himself. "I find them pretty heavy weather both for myself and for my patients," he said in an interview. . . .

The abortion live-birth dilemma has caught the attention of several experts on medical ethics, and they have proposed two possible solutions.

The simplest, advocated by Dr. Sissela Bok of the Harvard Medical School among others, is just to prohibit late abortions. Taking into account the possible errors in estimating gestational age, she argues, the cutoff should be set well before the earliest gestational age at which infants are surviving.

Using exactly this reasoning, several European countries—France and Sweden, for example—have made abortions readily available in the first three months of pregnancy but very difficult to get thereafter. The British, at the urging of Sir John Peel, an influential physician-statesman, have considered in each of the last three years moving the cutoff date from 28 weeks to 20 weeks, but so far have not done so.

But in this country, the Supreme Court has applied a different logic in defining the abortion right, and the groups that won that right would not cheerfully accept a retreat now.

A second approach, advocated by Mrs. Bok and others, is to define the woman's abortion right as being only a right to terminate the pregnancy, not to have the fetus dead. Then if the fetus is born live, it is viewed as a person in its own right, entitled to care appropriate to its condition.

This "progressive" principle is encoded in the policies

of many hospitals and the laws of some states, including New York and California. As the record shows, though, in the alarming event of an actual live birth, doctors on the scene may either observe the principle or ignore it. . . .

Of the various ways to perform an abortion after the midpoint of pregnancy, there is only one that never, ever results in live births.

It is D&E (dilation and evacuation), and not only is it foolproof, but many researchers consider it safer, cheaper and less unpleasant for the patient. However, it is particularly stressful to medical personnel. That is because D&E requires literally cutting the fetus from the womb and, then, reassembling the parts, or at least keeping them all in view, to assure that the abortion is complete.

Ten years ago it was considered reckless to do an abortion with cutting instruments after the first trimester of pregnancy. Now, improved instruments, more skilled practitioners and laminaria—bands of seaweed that expand when moist and are used to gently dilate the cervix, creating an opening through which to extract fetal parts—allow the technique to be used much later.

D&E is being hailed as extending the safe and easy techniques used for first-trimester abortions (cutting or vacuuming out the contents of the womb) well into the second three months of pregnancy. But there are dissenters. Dr. Bernard Nathanson, formerly a top New York City abortionist, now an anti-abortion author and lecturer, says that D&E "is a very dangerous technique in the hands of anyone less than highly skilled."

Besides, D&E puts all the emotional burden on the physicians. And there are other techniques that allow the doctor, as one physician put it, to "stick a needle in the [patient's] tummy," then leave the patient to deliver the fetus vaginally as normal childbirth and nurses to assist and clean up.

These more common methods for abortion after the midpoint of pregnancy use the instillation of either saline solution or prostaglandin. In these procedures, some of the woman's nurturing amniotic fluid is drawn out of the womb by an injection through her belly and is replaced with the abortion-inducing drug. (The amount of fluid in the womb is kept relatively constant to make sure the womb does not rupture.)

The two instillation substances work in different ways. Saline solution poisons the fetus, probably through ingestion, though the process is not completely understood. Usually within six hours, the fetal heartbeat stops. At the same time, the saline induces labor, though supplemental doses of other labor-inducing drugs often are given to speed this effect.

Prostaglandin, on the other hand, is a distillate of the chemical substance that causes muscles to move. It is thought not to affect the fetus directly but instead is potent at inducing labor. Fetal death, if it does occur, is from prematurity and the trauma of passage through the birth canal.

Each substance also has an undesired side effect. Saline, an anti-coagulant that increases bleeding, can make minor bleeding problems more serious and in rare cases even cause death. Prostaglandin, because it causes muscles to contract indiscriminately, was found to cause vomiting and diarrhea in more than half the patients in early tests. Claims that it causes fewer major complications, which made it preferred to saline by many in the mid-1970s, have now been questioned. And the high incidence of live births (40 times more frequent than with saline, according to one study) also has lessened its popularity.

But saline is not foolproof either in preventing live births. Dr. Thomas F. Kerenyi of Mt. Sinai Hospital in New York, the best-known researcher on saline abortions, said most live births result from "errors in techniques"— either administering too small a dosage or getting some of it into the wrong part of the womb.

A wrong estimation of gestational age can cause either a saline or prostaglandin abortion to fail. A larger-than-expected fetus might survive the trauma of labor or might reject a dose of saline (or urea, a third instillation substance sometimes used).

And on the basis of physical examination alone, studies show, doctors miss the correct gestational age by two weeks in one case out of five, by four weeks in one case out of 100, and sometimes by more than that. Pregnancies can be dated more exactly by a sonogram, a test that produces an outline image of the fetus in the womb, but because of its cost (about $100) many doctors continue to rely on physical exams.

There is one other abortion technique, hysterotomy, but it is the least desirable of all from several points of view. Because it is invasive surgery (identical to a Caesarean section), it has a much higher rate of complication than do the installation techniques. Usually done only after attempts to abort with saline have failed, it has the highest incidence of all of live births.

As the infant is lifted from the womb, said one obstetrician, "he is only sleeping, like his mother. She is under anesthesia, and so is he. You want to know how they kill him? They put a towel over his face so he can't breathe. And by the time they get him to the lab, he is dead." . . .

Nurses are the ones who bear the burden of handling the human-looking products of late abortions. And when an unintentional live birth occurs, they are the first to confront the waving of limbs and the gasping.

Reluctant to talk about their experiences, most of those interviewed for this article did not want their names to be published, and out of professional loyalty, they did not even want their hospitals to be named.

They spoke of being deeply troubled by what they have seen of late abortions in American hospitals.

Linda is a nurse in her late 50s in Southern California. Hurrying out of a patient's room one day to dispose of the aborted "tissue," as nurses were taught to think of it, she felt movement. Startled, she looked down, straight into the staring eyes of a live baby.

"It looked right at me," she recalled. "This baby had real big eyes. It looked at you like it was saying, 'Do something—do something.' Those haunting eyes. Oh God, I still remember them."

She rushed the 1½-pound infant to the nursing station. She took the heart rate—80 to 100 beats a minute. She timed the respirations—three to four breaths a minute. She called the doctor.

"I called him because the baby was breathing," Linda said. "It was pink. It had a heartbeat. The doctor told me the baby was not viable and to send it to the lab. I said, 'But it's breathing' and he said, 'It's non-viable, it won't be breathing long—send it to the lab.' "

She did not follow the order. Nor did she have re-sources at her command to provide any life-saving care. Two hours later the infant died, still at the nursing station, still without medical treatment. It died in a makeshift crib with one hot-water bottle for warmth and an open tube of oxygen blowing near its head.

The nursing supervisor, Linda said, had refused to let her put the baby in the nursery, where there was equip-ment to assist premature babies in distress. "She said to follow the doctor's orders and take it to the lab. I kept it with me at the station. We couldn't do an awful lot for it."

This happened eight years ago, in 1973, but Linda is still upset. "I stood by and watched that baby die without doing a thing," she said. "I have guilt feelings to this day. I feel the baby might have lived had it been properly cared for."

What do you think Jesus would have said of all this?

If the image of babies brought into the world with their skin burned from the abortionist's saline injection but still crying out for life cannot touch our hearts, *then we really are no better than Nazis.* If we turn away from this sight without taking action, then we are accessories to the doctors who smother those appeals for life. The article suggests that to solve this "problem" of babies who live, abortions should be performed "earlier." That the baby aborted "earlier" is the same living child as the one aborted a few weeks later is never addressed. The real point is that abortion was, is, and always will be a crime, and its pre-sent superficial legality cannot undo this fact.

The prolife movement has accomplished a great deal

in making people aware of the solid scientific evidence about the unborn and their full humanity. Proabortion advocates today cannot blithely refer to a fetus as nothing more than a collection of tissue: people know better. But that does not necessarily mean that the prolife movement will succeed in reversing the *Roe* v. *Wade* decision through legislative means. For, as some of us have suspected, the *issue has never really been, for many proabortion advocates, whether the fetus is a human being.* As prolife educational efforts affect more and more people, those in favor of abortion have started to change tactics. An article in *Newsweek,* January 11, 1982, entitled "But Is It a Person?" reviews the striking evidence for defining a fetus as a human being; it concludes, however, on a different note:

> Even many doctors who believe that abortions are justified will concede that life begins at fertilization, and that the fetus becomes human at any point the anti-abortion groups care to specify; the problem is not determining when "actual human life" begins, but when the value of that life begins to outweigh other considerations, such as the health, or even the happiness, of the mother. And on that question, science is silent [p. 44].

But the question *was* when actual human life begins. At this key point we must not let the brutal humanistic elite change the rules. We must see that, instead of admitting the error of his thinking, here again the secularist will be willing to press on in opposition to the truth, as he has pressed on despite the lessons of the humanistic failures through history. In other words, once again they don't play by their own rules of rationality. For years the argument was, "Well, you can't tell when life begins." Now, as science uncovers more and more of the complexities of developing babies, comes the switch to, "Well, so it's a person, so what? What we're interested in is the happiness of the mother." Gone allusions to humanness, even the hardship cases; now apparently it all comes down to "happiness." Life and liberty seem to have gone by the board.

Is this a double standard? Of course. Can they get away with it? In view of the silent church they may well.

In this matter of convenient short memories, we have come to the same place as official party doctrine in the Soviet Union. There history is changed on a day-to-day basis as the needs of state dictate. Like Newspeak in *1984,* truth is that set of "facts" that for that day serve the government interests. So it is with the liberal humanist's past claims and arguments; they are abandoned in favor of new ones as soon as they prove obsolete. And with a society whose memory is about as long as a lobotomized lobster, past claims are never compared to the present realities anyway.

The humanist death machine is driven by people who often occupy prestigious and powerful positions. For example, those involved in the *Hard Choices* project are all respected academicians or members of the PBS media. The project itself was supported by the National Endowment for the Humanities: *that means public tax dollars, yours and mine, contributed to the dissemination of the message that God is dead and therefore we must hail the social engineer Caesars.* All of this under the aegis of "neutral" and "balanced" public affairs programming. Meanwhile, the networks are largely closed (except on a do-it-yourself basis) to the Judeo-Christian view.

I'd be hard pressed to come up with an organization that epitomizes the hard-nosed duplicity of those who benefit from the myth of neutrality more than Planned Parenthood. Federally funded, Planned Parenthood practices the most hypocritical perversion of the principle of not letting one's right hand know what the left is doing. Planned Parenthood speaks of sexual morality only as a "personal choice," dispensing the means of birth control to young people without parental knowledge or consent, creating the impression that sex is nothing more than good healthy fun, that it doesn't have psychological or physical consequences; then they turn around and bemoan the present epidemic of venereal disease, the rise of unwanted teenage pregnancies, and the suicides that often result. They can't, for the life of them, see the connection!

Planned Parenthood and groups like them merrily claim that they are against "legislating morality" even as they draw on public funds and lobby intensely to legislate *their* immorality. In 1981 they spent 3.7 million dollars for legislative and "public education" programs to defend legalized abortion and to preserve federal funding of their clinics.[3]

Planned Parenthood's most consistent claim is that it does not use federal money to fund abortion. This is probably technically true. But the family-planning centers of Planned Parenthood operate in conjunction with medical clinics, *which do* perform abortions. Planned Parenthood's propaganda helps to convince women to have abortions, so their claim is rather like a pimp saying he has nothing to do with prostitution.

This "neutral organization"[4] that wouldn't dream of legislating morality can send out a fund-raising letter, in order to fight the Human Life Amendment, which uses reactionary language that corroborates the argument of this book so expressly that it would verge on parody if I had made it up:

> If the amendment passes Congress . . . the New Right and their radical religious allies will have succeeded in forcing you to live your life and plan your family the *way* they think you should. *They will have accomplished that which our Founding Fathers so greatly feared: they will have merged church and state and imposed their prejudices on the entire country, thus eliminating religious freedom as we know it. All this despite the*

fact that 80 percent of Americans oppose prohibition of abortion.
[The author's, Fay Wattleton's, emphasis, not mine.]

The self-appointed moralists believe that an unwanted pregnancy—with all its implications and potential complications—is the penalty that must be exacted from a woman for an act of love. Because after all, isn't punishment due—aren't women to blame for stirring up sinful thoughts in the hearts of men? It is a vision of the Dark Ages, of the Inquisition, of a time no person—man or woman—should have to face.

The hysterical and paranoid quote from the Planned Parenthood Newsletter above would be almost amusing if it were not for the reality of the situation that they, and others like them, have created. The theory: "free speech," "choice," "freedom of conscience"; the practice: the staring eyes of the maimed and battered baby of a late-term abortion. The fact that there is so little accountability demanded of these great theoreticians of "liberty," "freedom" and "choice," in terms of the reality they have produced, further illustrates the myth of neutrality and the double standard of this generation. The media, always hooked on the words and slogans of such groups as Planned Parenthood and faithfully ready to report their accusations against the "new right" or whoever else dares to oppose them, nevertheless look askance at the realities they produce. When was the last time you saw a photograph in a major American newspaper of the types of abortions being performed, described in the long quote in this chapter? And yet our media pride themselves on revealing everything to the people, do they not?

The double standard and hypocrisy in sexual attitudes confronts us everywhere. I remember sitting in a Los Angeles hotel room watching a local talk show. The host and his guest were discussing a halfway house that had been established for runaway teenage prostitutes in the Hollywood area. An interview with Hugh Hefner's daughter, who helps her father run Playboy Enterprises, followed. The commentator lauded her for Playboy Enterprises' commitment to underwrite the finances for this halfway house.

Playboy Enterprises, the epitome of anti-women sexism, of course, has probably done more to create the climate of sexual permissiveness and exploitation of women as sex objects than any other group. The playboy mentality helped to put those teenage prostitutes on the streets in the first place. I expected someone, *sometime,* to point out this barn-sized irony. But no one did: a sickening example of the myth of neutrality we're talking about.

Dick Leggett, editor of *New Wine* magazine, had this to say about the culture's understanding of sexuality:

> The message is this: "Morality brings misery." . . .
> . . . This presumptuous humanistic assertion that "morality brings misery" is a gigantic lie. Morality doesn't bring misery—*immorality* (or amorality) does. Even a cursory glance at history and sociological statistics confirms that immorality in marriage and the family brings wreckage and trauma to this pillar of all social structure; immorality in business wreaks economic and ethical havoc; and immorality in government brings disrepute and ultimate downfall to men and nations. The debris of broken human lives strewn across the face of the earth is not the ruins of morality run amuck, but rather the wreckage left by repeated whirlwinds of immorality and anarchy. Morality has not spawned this present misery—the *lack of it* has.
> But immorality is not only destructive—it is also unproductive. In simple terms, it just doesn't work.

The myth of neutrality holds that the Judeo-Christian principles governing sexual conduct are restrictive and joyless, whereas the opposite is true. Within the judicious boundaries given to us by a wise and loving Creator, we find the *freedom* to be human: freedom to care for others in ways that they can depend on and trust in; freedom to love in a way which makes others free; freedom to fight for life and compassion. Christianity is Life! It is joy! It is warmth, comfort, consolation, and humanness!

This is full Life. It is the mean-spirited, selfish, so-called liberated sexual world that is narrow and confining to the human spirit. Yes, it provides a sort of "freedom." The same freedom experienced by a person thrown naked and bleeding into a tank full of piranhas! *Freedom to be eaten alive* by the selfish sterility of a twentieth-century "relationship." Freedom to kill one's offspring, which is barbarism per se. Instead, Christian morality offers the warm sweetness of permanent, unconditional love. A love that at times must also be expressed in outrage at those who would murder, rape, and pillage the human race, albeit in the name of "humanity," "choice," and "progress."

The issue of life is not some abstract national debate to be dabbled in, but a life and death struggle with the forces of evil. A fight to be won.

6 / Science, Medicine, and the Politics of Death

If there is any branch of the ruling elite in today's world that consistently presents itself as "neutral" and therefore reasonable, pluralistic, and enlightened, it is science.

But far from neutrality, the science of today contains a liberal humanistic bias as twisted as the bigotry of the media.

Since science is fashionable today, it allows its fraternity to propose cloddish monstrosities as a solution to man's problems in many fields. Fashion rules and, anyway, who but the experts can even dare to speak up?

Much as the defense at the Nuremberg trials was often "I was only obeying orders," so today we disown our responsibilities as human beings if we are afraid to appear unfashionable under the guise of "What can one person do?" or "What can we say; after all, the experts have agreed . . ." Only such copouts, prompted by the evangelical inferiority complex of institutions and individuals, can explain the deafening silence on many fronts concerning the agenda of much of modern "science."

What is this agenda? It is an agenda of death as a solution to problems real or, as in the case of the diminishing resource argument, *imagined*. An agenda based on philosophy, *not* science. Its neutrality is of the same quality as that of the Pol Pot regime of Cambodian infamy.

The philosophy of science of any age influences, to a great extent, the achievements of science in that period and its ethics.[1] Science is inherently philosophical in that only certain kinds of world views allow the very idea of science, the pursuit of knowledge and power through observation, to arise. Modern western science is the product of Renaissance and Reformational views of the creation. Since the earth and all that was in it were formed by God, whose mind was reasonable, orderly, and consistent, and since man was made in His image (because he thought along the same lines as God), man could base his pursuit of knowledge on the basis that the creation would be like its Creator: reasonable, orderly, and consistent.

But while modern science came into being because of this view, the humanistic scientist of today has rejected the Christian conception of nature. William B. Provine, writing in the *Hard Choices* magazine, addresses this point:

> Judaism and Christianity maintain the belief that a single divinity designed the world and everything in it and then gave moral laws to humanity.[2]
>
> Plato, Aristotle, Christ and their successors did not have to contradict the evidence of their senses to arrive at this position. The belief in a grand design shaping both the physical world and ethics was based on abundant, obvious, and emotionally satisfying evidence: regularities of the heavenly bodies, patterns in animals and plants, and the existence of human reason. . . . Belief in overarching order was dominant; it can be seen as easily in such scientists as Newton, Harvey, Einstein as in the theologians Augustine, Luther and Tillich. But beginning with Darwin, biology has undermined this view. Darwin in effect asserted that all living organisms had been created by a combination of chance and necessity—natural selection. . . .
>
> Nearly every field of biology has contributed evidence that the process of evolution works by *a consistent set of purposeless rules.* . . .
>
> Except for the laws of probability and cause and effect, there is no organizing principle in the world and no purpose. Thus, there are no moral or ethical laws that

belong to the nature of things, no absolute guiding principles for human society [my emphasis, p. 3].

Only a scientist utterly committed to pseudo-philosophi-
cal deception could make such a narrow statement. Yet
Provine's views are widely shared, as are his motivations.
If the rules which govern the universe are "purposeless" or
random, how then, at the same time, can they be "consistent"?[3]

That Provine and those like him find themselves
arrayed against the views of "Plato, Aristotle, Christ and
their successors . . . Newton, Harvey, Einstein . . . Augustine, Luther, Tillich" but are not given pause by this
only further demonstrates the absurdity of their assumptions. Provine and other scientists who agree with him
foolishly over-stress the element of chance. We can be
certain that the scientists involved in the Apollo project did
not share Provine's simplistic chance theories since success
in landing their spacecraft within inches of their desig-
nated, pre-plotted landing site required the most rigorous
and exacting planning and calculation. Indeed, scientists,
despite statements to the contrary like Provine's, *still by
necessity operate on the basis of assumptions which embrace and
depend upon the orderly conduct of nature.*[4] If they really believed only in chance and randomness, they could never
trust the results of their much touted experiments. The
world, having come here by chance, and proceeding on a
disorderly path little understood, could never produce
consistent and meaningful test results. In other words,
their most basic assumption is wrong.

But modern science rarely admits to the whopping
contradiction in its own reasoning. It plays down the
traditions it has inherited, the Newtons, Harveys, and
even the Einsteins and their "quaint beliefs."

Why? The humanistic contemporary philosophy of
science has many advantages to those who would like to

play God. Provine is right to point to Darwin as his mentor. His evolutionary theory, divorced from any concept of divine guidance, made legitimate the tremendous brutality of the Industrial Revolution by making the "survival of the fittest" appear right and good. (The industrialist had thousands of workers under his boot; that was okay, for he was the "most fit.") The same philosophy undergirded the race war of the Nazis. And in our own day there are those, like Mr. Provine, who are using it to justify the pro-death abortion and infanticide neo-fascist movement. The parent is the stronger or more "fit"; the stronger dictates. The woman can verbalize, so it is "her body" which is to be respected. The parent can talk to the judge; the child cannot. Therefore, why bother missing a night's sleep over the starvation of a child?

Thus, science and medicine are not and cannot be neutral or considered above morality. The philosophy upon which scientists base their work has very specific effects in what types of technologies grow out of scientific research. Separated from Judeo-Christian origins, medical science can assume monstrous dimensions. We are all familiar with the drastic changes and theories of potential doom brought about by the invention of the atom bomb. *But there are other inventions which pose a more immediate and real threat,* which are responsible for mass death, *NOW.*

To be specific, take the prostaglandin drugs being worked on by the Upjohn Company. This multinational conglomerate is engaged in a worldwide effort of epic proportions in its quest to make abortion a "home remedy" for unwanted life. The only modern equivalent to their activity is that of Farban, I.E. who, in the 1930s and '40s, produced the fatal poison gas Cyclone B for the Nazis in Germany. Upjohn may well, through its prostaglandin drugs, take far more lives than the combined efforts of all modern pharmaceutical production have saved. And only the bias of a liberal, humanistic press could cover up such a fact for *so long*. Worldwide abortion takes more lives annually than some of the "worst case" scenarios of nuclear war!

I say "so long" because Upjohn started this incredible program *before* the advent of legalized permissive abortion in 1973. They were planning ahead, so to speak, anticipating consumer demand. And like all good corporate marketers, they are now busily helping to create the "need" for their product.

Freelance journalist Dexter Duggan, in two articles prepared for the *Moral Majority Report,* August 24 and September 21, 1981, detailed the "progress" which Upjohn Company was making in this field of wholesale drug-induced abortion. Here are some excerpts.

> A longtime dream of abortion advocates is to reduce "terminating a pregnancy" to a matter almost as routine as taking an aspirin. . . .
>
> . . . Moreover, motivation for abortion might be increased if a woman came to view the matter as about as simple as drinking a cup of tea.
>
> Although there are already approximately 1.5 million permissive abortions in the nation annually, groups like Planned Parenthood say this figure isn't high enough and that hundreds of thousands of more abortions are required for the "unmet need." . . .[5]
>
> . . . "In 1968, Earl S. Gerard, M.D., now Upjohn Research Manager, Fertility Research, and others began to examine the frequency of abortion and methods used to perform them," according to a special edition in 1980 of the company publication, Upjohn INTER-VIEW.
>
> The special edition continued: "In the U.S.," Gerard said, "it didn't seem to make a lot of difference if a particular state had a 'liberalized' abortion law such as the one in New York. We had to conclude that physicians considered some abortions as medically valid procedures. We then set out to give those physicians a safe and effective tool."

This statement appears to say, in other words, that if some doctors wanted to do abortions, regardless of state laws, Upjohn was ready to perfect and sell them the "tool" they needed.

Not satisfied to rest on past performance, Upjohn today is pushing ahead with development of a new generation of abortion drugs. Experiments are underway in Nashville involving the 15-methyl prostaglandin F2 methyl ester suppository, for use earlier in pregnancy. . . .

. . . Meharry, an institution with a very strong identification as a black facility, was chosen to help perfect a new abortion procedure. . . .

. . . Meharry Medical College and Hubbard Hospital are located together in a large black area of Nashville. One local physician told me that Hubbard primarily treats black patients. Referring to who the subjects might be for the abortion suppository research, he said, "If it's at Meharry, you've got to have a lot of blacks."

Many blacks, including civil rights leader, the Rev. Jesse Jackson, have charged at various times that blacks and other minorities have been targeted for "genocide" by promotion of permissive abortion among them.

Supreme Court Justice Harry Blackmun, who wrote the Court's original permissive abortion decisions and continues to vote on the pro-abortion side in further cases considered by the Court, has said "the cancer of poverty will continue to grow if abortion can't be applied as a cure for the social problems of the poor."

Blackmun's is only one of many similar voices that claim the children of the poor, rather than inequitable economic factors, are the cause of poverty.

Apparently due to social pressures exerted by figures like Harry Blackmun, it is a fact that blacks are aborting in America in disproportionately high numbers to whites. . . .

. . . Although considerable testing remains to be done before it would be known whether the suppositories would be approved for the American market, Upjohn is dedicated to expanding its sales whenever possible, overseas as well as domestically.

In a *Tennessee Register* story, Patricia Frazier Harmon wrote: "In Upjohn's annual report for the year 1979, the company indicated that ultimate targets for massive release of the (prostaglandin suppository) drug will be the Third World countries, China, India and the Eastern European bloc nations. . . .

. . . Often in its own defense, Upjohn uses language that suggests the giant drug company is somehow forced to make abortion drugs.

Because abortionists want the drugs.

Because poor people want abortions.

For any of a variety of reasons that sounds as if kind-hearted Upjohn doesn't have the willpower to turn down any request.

However, pro-lifers say, Upjohn's major motivation is hope of substantial worldwide profits. The pro-lifers say that although prostaglandin substances could be developed in a number of beneficial ways to treat the real ills of humankind, Upjohn has focused on the destructive abortion potential of this remarkable substance.

Upjohn's exploding abortion market couldn't really get off the ground in the United States until the High Court gave abortion the green light, the pro-lifers say. Ratification of a strong Human Life Amendment is the only way to put this destructive genie back in the bottle and force Upjohn—a company that talks about being forced to work on abortion—to work only on life-saving, life-enhancing products again. . . .

Referring to Upjohn's abortion involvement, one source in Kalamazoo[6] told me that while the company "is sensitive to protest, it is also callous to it" because Upjohn figures the protests will fade away. "For years," the source said, "Upjohn has sent out the same blah-blah" in response to letters of protest. "Upjohn thinks, whenever a new wave of protest crests, just hang on and it will dribble out." But in the last couple years, as more Protestants have become informed about the issue, "that's resulted in a real flood of mail that they got very concerned about." . . .

. . . Dr. Hubbard said in his address to the prostaglandin researchers at Upjohn:

"Finally, there is the problem of abortion. It would be quaint if we had no concerns about discussing here the limitation of life when the profession of medicine and the pharmaceutical industry have historically devoted themselves to the preservation of life. We have to examine the rationale for this endeavor.

"We are confronted with the problem of discrepancy between total productivity of the human race as it is now organized and its consumptive demands. This discrepancy has led to a threatening difference between the 'have's' and 'have-nots.' If we are to have each human life fulfill its potential, then we will have to reduce this discrepancy between productivity and consumptive demand.

"With limited resources in an ecology that is subject to harmful alteration, there is some doubt about the strategy of only increasing production. Therefore, for the first time, the medical profession is involved in the inhibition of life and here we look to the most effective and convenient means. . . ."

Dr. Hubbard summed up: "This symposium addressed with hope three broad concerns: how industry and academia shall work fruitfully together; how we shall develop useful application in human reproduction of a new class of therapeutic compounds; how we shall deal with the logic and technology of the limitation of life. The success already achieved suggests a most promising future." . . .

Among other interesting aspects about Upjohn's alliance with the promotion of abortion is the fact that the same major public relations firm in New York City represents both Upjohn and the Planned Parenthood Federation of America. It is Manning, Selvage and Lee, Inc., of New York.

Even a United Press International editor, Patricia McCormack, commented on the obvious abortion connection. Two years ago, in a story about the dispute between prolifers and abortion advocates, McCormack noted:

"The (Planned Parenthood) Federation choice of Manning, Selvage and Lee will place the public relations firm in the position of helping both clients, the Federation and Upjohn, since anything done to preserve abortion-on-demand works to keep up Upjohn's abortion medicine business."

And Upjohn appears fully aware of massive profits to be made from such sales.

Upjohn's 1979 Annual Report, pointing to "a decade of growth unprecedented in its history with record sales and earnings," was enthusiastic for the future: "Enormous potential markets for contraceptives and abortifacients exist in India and China." For the first time since World War II, the annual report said, Upjohn was engaged in "significant activity" in India—the sale of an injectable abortifacient, Prostin/15M.

The annual report said that during the decade, Upjohn's sales of all products had shot up from approximately $400 million to $1.5 billion. (A subsequent story in the *Kalamazoo Gazette* said Upjohn President Dr. William N. Hubbard Jr. forecast $3 billion in sales by 1985 and over $5 billion by 1990.)

In some places in Upjohn's 1979 annual report, a tone of hard-sell strategy comes through that might sound more appropriate to a used car lot. Speaking of Upjohn's financial condition, the report said:

"We achieved these results through continued market penetration, reflecting greater demand worldwide for our products, and through our intensified efforts to maintain earnings in an environment of increasing inflationary pressures."

The rather callous-sounding heading, "Business Opportunities in Human Health," appeared in the report. Listed among these business opportunities were abortion opportunities. . . .

A few years earlier, fears over recombinant DNA work by scientists in general had made headlines as people expressed concern over the possibility of the creation of dangerous new life forms. . . .

And, considering Upjohn's previous decisions to ignore life-and-death questions of morality involving issues like massive abortion, people may not feel exactly comfortable with the idea that the same company is working actively in other areas involving powerful ethical questions and nightmare-like fears. . . .

. . . Last year, the San Diego *Union* newspaper featured a story on pioneer California abortionist Dr. Edward Allred, who is regarded as "Mr. Abortion" by many Californians. Dr. Allred was quoted about the future use of the abortion suppository:

"When the suppository is available at every drug store, I'll be a dinosaur. I'll be glad to get out of the business. I'm sure I'll be remembered as a pioneer. I love what I've created, and I love my organization."

These excerpts from the two-part series by Dexter Duggan expose without question the ugly presence of the myth of neutrality in science. *This is "science" with an anti-life agenda with a vengeance!*

The most horrifying aspect of the prostaglandin drugs may be their "sanitary" nature. Even to those who accept the idea of abortion-on-demand for one ill-founded reason or another, few can think about an abortionist without a sense of revulsion. The man who does the deed, literally as well as figuratively, has blood on his hands. But this reaction and the misgivings it provokes will be done away with by the new drugs. Killing a human being manually takes a lot of effort and can be quite messy, but the prostaglandin suppository will suit our deodorized, hair spray, hygiene-junky society perfectly. What could be more convenient for a generation, a century, hooked on genocide?[7]

Out of sight, out of mind. Few poor people vote, and by the time a full-scale genocide has been carried out against the poor, the black, and all those other non-persons, we won't even know they have ever been here.

Poverty leaves few monuments for posterity. The grass hut in Africa, the shanty town on the outskirts of Calcutta, the tenement buildings of the south Bronx will disappear without a trace.

Only the rich leave monuments. Like the tourists who tramp over the Parthenon in Greece and see the Coliseum in Rome, perhaps someday the executive mansions of those who run the Upjohn Company will be sites of historical interest. They will be remembered as the "benefactors" who "solved the world's problems of hunger, poverty, and disease for all of us." How pleasant to know that they became rich while performing such mighty acts of benevolence.

After World War I there was a widespread feeling of anger against the profiteers who had capitalized on the war, turning the fighting into a giant, international business fueled by their munitions. But their place in history will pale when compared with the massive pharmaceutical conglomerates, as they embrace the secularistic, amoral doctrine of death as an expedient solution to mankind's problems. If, that is, anyone chooses to see through the benign appearances to the cancerous reality.

The signs of current events indicate hardly anyone will. For the terrifying reality of *1984* is already in significant respects with us. Michele Vink, reporting on "Abortion and Birth Control in Canton, China" in the *Wall Street Journal* (Monday, November 30, 1981), reviews the policies and how they are carried out in the birth control program China began in 1979. China has instituted contracts that a married couple can sign with the government which reward the couple for having only one child.

> A couple that signs a contract . . . will have a greater living space. It will receive a wide variety of financial benefits, including extra ration coupons, free education and health care for the child, salary increases—and the approval of the street committee, the important local branch of the Communist Party. . . .
>
> If a couple has a second or third child, however, penalties begin. The family will lose all benefits gained under the one-child plan and, in fact, must pay them back.

An extra child will receive no free medical benefits or allowance supplements. A third child will receive no ration coupons and his family's rations will be reduced. His parents will suffer a 10% decrease in wages and possible loss of promotional opportunities at work. And because every pregnancy must have the approval of the mother's work unit, a woman who dares have a child outside the accepted birth plan leaves herself vulnerable to criticism from important local cadres.

The "approval of the street committee" and "criticism" from local cadres make the actual practice of this nightmarish program worse, much worse. Vink says that reporters have seen pregnant women rounded up in trucks and taken to hospitals for abortions. It doesn't matter what stage the pregnancy is in, either.

Though doctors aren't supposed to perform abortions past the eighth month of pregnancy, they do, a Chinese doctor reports. "Every day hundreds of fetuses arrive at the morgue," he says. A woman with an unauthorized pregnancy is likely to receive an injection from hospital doctors before labor, resulting in a stillborn child or a baby so ill that it dies in a few days, the source adds. There are even reports of infanticide in city hospitals, with doctors killing babies immediately after birth if they are third children.

In the countryside sterilizations sometimes are forced rather than accepted voluntarily. A peasant from Domen County in Guangdong reported that since 1976 women who bear three children "must" be sterilized.

Finally, Vink quotes a top Communist Party official as saying, "We must mobilize all those whose pregnancies aren't covered by the plan to take remedial measures." Butchery is what he means by "remedial measures," of course.

We might at this point be tempted to comfort ourselves with the thought that these things happen only in the Nazi Germanys and Chinas and other totalitarian states. We have already, however, aborted more babies than Hitler killed Jews. But if someone would find "population control" on this scale offensive in a way he does not abortion-on-demand, he should be aware that the social engineers in our own society have already begun to advance a line of reasoning which is in total accord with the policies of China today. Writing on eugenics in the *Hard Choices* magazine, William B. Provine, that charter member of our brave new world, considers the question of whether an abortion should be legally required if a baby is discovered to have Down's syndrome.

> At present the answer is clearly no. Yet there is no reason to believe that won't change. Laws requiring, say, driver's licenses limit individual rights. Laws restricting the number of children, or requiring the abortion of an afflicted fetus seem unlikely now, but thirty years ago, it would have seemed incredible that the Supreme Court would ever permit abortion. . . .[8]
>
> . . . As natural resources become scarcer and the standard of living begins to decline, "wasting" resources to maintain seriously defective individuals may come to seem immoral. . . .
>
> If resources become severely limited, we may also see a time when licenses are required for child-bearing and when abortions or sterilization are demanded in some situations. And when scarcity is a fact of life, such laws may come to be seen as highly moral and disobedience regarded as vicious and anti-social [p. 10].

Provine obviously does not disapprove enacting such laws, or mandating them as a member of the future social engineering elite to which our government will have to turn because life in a fully "scientifically and technologically advanced" culture will be "too complex" for the person of average intellect to rule. The fact that we mere mortals are inclined to treat our house plants with more concern than these new "social engineers" would give to human beings is dismissed by the elite as mere sentimentality on the part of the uninitiated. Note also that, with an "on-again, off-again" morality, Provine plays both sides well. First saying that "there are no ethical or moral laws," he now conveniently says that laws regulating who will be born "may come to be seen as highly moral," and thus he really has his cake and eats it, too!

Are there other Provines? In an article entitled, "China's Birth Limits Praised," which ran in the *Chicago Sun-Times,* on Thursday, December 17, 1981, the Associated Press reviewed the latest world population study by the U. S. Census Bureau. It "reported the worldwide rate of population growth declined in the 1970s, *thanks largely to China's efforts to limit births.*" [My emphasis.] Whoever sits on the Census Bureau must surely know *how* China has limited births; to issue a study which, in the *Sun-Times* evaluation (it was their headline) "praises" China's efforts is like talking about population decreases for Eastern European Jews during the holocaust and praising a "significant decline." I can hardly see this matter as just an oversight. Such examples of Newspeak, or a version of the truth which serves ulterior motives, suggest that many in government care only about their own power over the individual and nothing about the preservation of humane values.

A friend of mine, over lunch one day, spoke of the sinking feeling he inevitably gets when each new idea lessening the worth of individuals is put forth. He spoke of the fact that, like abortion, no matter how inhuman or even inane the idea, he gets the sinking feeling because he knows that once it is being espoused by the elite, it is only a matter of time until it is accepted.

The reason for this is, of course, that in the absence of a firm moral standard each "idea," however implausible, gains credence. It is a case of the morally incompetent teaching the morally blind. Ideas of controlling poverty or whatever by mass death that would have been robustly rejected in times past are now "seriously considered" by those pundits who are idly sitting on the wall and watching as mildly interested spectators as their culture disintegrates.

Strange contradictions come forth in such times. On the one hand, we look to science and technology to solve our problems, but on the other, we place so little faith in their advance that we revert to the crudest and most archaic of all solutions—death—to solve problems.

So science scoffingly rejects Christian ethics as unequal to the task of providing leadership, but itself looks not to new inventions to fill the gap but instead reverts to barbaric tactics like murder to solve, say, a problem of food distribution, albeit in the name of "population control." So, like some strange figure of mythology, modern humanistic liberal man and science treat our culture like an ogre in a tale in which he has a beautiful, talented wife whom he will neither talk to or sleep with, and keeps her locked in a tower to prevent anyone else from doing so. Just so, the liberal humanist continues to cut the Christian voice of compassion out of the process and can himself only point to death dressed in various forms—abortion—euthanasia—etc. as a "solution." This surely cannot be seen as either good science *or* ethics.

The terms or bases upon which debate in our society is carried on increasingly assume that God, and thus the Judeo-Christian tradition, are irrelevant. The Almighty does not even enter into the discussion, and in the priggish and unenlightened closed box of secular humanism, where the state and the individual are the only realities, where the sky has been blotted out by secular absolutist government, the most monstrous of solutions can be proposed. And if we are unable to restore God and His life-giving law to the world of these discussions, place Him back on His throne above the state and the courts, then the "practical" solutions of the neo-fascist engineers appear as inevitable as their callous proponents would like to suggest. As an example of this "new," totally secularized thinking (not really new when one thinks about it: Rome with its rulers like Caligula and Nero insisted its sovereigns were god; so did ancient Egypt and many other pagan civilizations), Harry Schwartz, writing in the "My Turn" section of *Newsweek*, February 8, 1982, expresses the following opinion:

> It is time for us to bite the bullet and begin debating explicitly how we are going to ration health care. I know the topic is unpleasant, and we'd all prefer it to go away. But it won't vanish, and we have no good alternative. . . .
>
> . . . In 1982 we will almost certainly spend more than $300 billion for health care and exceed 10 percent of the GNP if we continue on our present mindless course. . . .
>
> What . . . forms of rationing are possible, then? . . .
>
> . . . Economists have suggested banning government or private insurance systems that pay for care in simple and limited illnesses. . . .
>
> A second alternative might be a decision to deny free care to individuals for whom there is no good future, like Karen Quinlan. Thus only hospice care—emphasizing relief from pain and tranquility of atmosphere—might be offered to patients older than, say, 85, or to younger patients suffering from diseases that are clearly hopeless, for example, amyotrophic lateral sclerosis, better known as Lou Gehrig's disease. Expensive and heroic medical care might also be denied to those unfortunate babies born with Down's syndrome, or serious spina bifida or other ailments. . . .

Mr. Schwartz, identified by *Newsweek* as a "writer-in-residence at the College of Physicians and Surgeons of Columbia University," exemplifies the attitude of the humanistic secularist at the end of the twentieth century in dealing with human suffering. First and most importantly, he has eliminated the idea of vocation—which implies Christian charity, duty, and compassion—from his set of references; and therefore he is left with only "economic solutions." In other words, to a Mr. Schwartz the idea of medicine and the care of others as a vocation or duty simply does not exist. Gone the idea of Mother Theresa and the Sisters of Charity and all the other orders and religious groups who have provided medical care for centuries at a greatly reduced cost because they view their work as a ministry. Gone the idea of the physician as a healer who has become a doctor, not to become rich, but, would you believe it, to alleviate suffering.

Perhaps, as a writer-in-residence at a college of physicians, since his livelihood depends on the medical profession, Mr. Schwartz therefore does not dare to suggest that one way to reduce medical costs would be to limit the greed and avarice of a medical profession that, in relation to the rest of society, already earns incredible financial rewards.

Another thing to notice about the Mr. Schwartzes of the world and their intolerant views is that the "eighty-five year olds" and infants are always the ones to be denied medical care and thus eliminated. That there is no call for eliminating medical health care for the writers-in-residence of this world or, say, doctors (Schwartz says there are too many) highlights that the secular humanist, despite his rhetoric of compassion, will turn first to the weak and defenseless on which to exercise his deadly theories. Talk of the "quality of life," etc. becoming a smoke screen for eliminating the burdensome!

The myth of neutrality comes in here very clearly when one considers the godlike fiat which characterizes the statements of Mr. Schwartz. First, a statement of "fact" that, to him and for his purposes, cannot be disputed: the present trend in medicine is a "mindless course" (this business of caring for people). All discussion of ethics, right and wrong, good and evil, ends there before he *begins* to argue. The discussion then proceeds on the basis of economics, which are deliberately divorced from the heritage of western man, the heritage of discussing human problems in terms of an ethics of compassion *before* economics, with the exception of those dark moments such as the rationalization of the slave trade. Still Mr. Schwartz presents himself as the voice of reason and amiable respectability, in contrast to the dangerous prolife advocates who espouse such reactionary views as "Let the little fella live." Yet what he describes as "hospice care" amounts to centers for euthanasia, which closely parallel the death centers descibed in *Brave New World*.

Indeed, only by studiously avoiding the lessons which the literary and humane voices in our culture have been trying to teach us throughout this gloomy century can "modest proposals" like those of Mr. Schwartz be put forward. *Most astonishing of all, given the reasonable assumption that journalists have some background in the humanities, is that a national magazine would give space to such neo-fascist opinions, with no comment.* And would at the same time routinely refuse to cover and give space to such "reactionary right-wing extreme" ideas as the preciousness of life!

The predictions of *1984, Brave New World,* and those in C. S. Lewis's space trilogy *have come to pass.* When all questions are decided on the basis of economics alone, when man can no longer appeal to God or even transcendent ideals, but is subject to the absolute control of the state, life is and will become more and more barbarous and bleak. It is no longer a question of where things *will* go. We are there *now!*

Contemplate the unexplored "liberal" uses for the prostaglandin death drugs. For a start, the South Africans could resolve their problem of racial imbalance in a generation; the whites could quite happily give the vote to each and every surviving black man, once a program, let us say, of "therapeutic, retroactive, racial-equality fertility control" had taken place. A little prostaglandin in the water supply: "vitamins" to the tribal homeland for the good of the "colored peoples."

The Soviet Union, following China's lead, could solve in ten years its traditional problems with the Moslem peoples along its southern borders, and the Christian church.

What a team Khadafy and the scientific researchers of Upjohn will make together!

And if we can see these things happening in other parts of the world, what will happen when eugenics give our economic competitors "real advantages" in the marketplace? How long will our Judeo-Christian traditions prevail against the "voices of reason" in our own society which urge us to "be realistic" and forge ahead with the anti-human agenda of the future, especially if such advances are highly profitable? After all, why not Harlem? Why not the Bronx? Supreme Court justices have already seen abortion as a means of dealing with the poor. In his reasoning on abortion, Justice Blackmun refers to "demographic considerations" and the like.

A hue and cry arose after the Second World War because the railroad tracks to Auschwitz were never bombed by the allies, even though they knew that hundreds of thousands of Jews and Slovaks were being transported by them to their deaths. I wonder how future generations (if there are any) will regard those of us with Judeo-Christian principles today if we do not respond to the holocaust in our own time. The insanity of the Upjohns and the social engineers and the purveyors of economic final solutions *must be stopped!*

A myth of neutrality? Yes. A conspiracy? No. Something much worse than a conspiracy. With a conspiracy one could find the conspirators and do something about them individually. But what we are talking about here is a way of thinking as pervasive as it is pernicious. Worse, a fashionable way of thinking. Many who occupy leadership positions in our society are mesmerized, like rabbits looking into the headlights of an oncoming car, by their vision of themselves as God. Such phrases as "The scholars agree" have replaced "Thus saith the Lord" as the absolute final word. These people all think the same way, and so they will all act the same way. They have the same vested interest in proving themselves "right" and Judeo-Christian thinkers "wrong," and they share the same provincialism and bigotry in considering all other opinions, especially those which endorse the moral absolutes of Christianity.

We are up against a monolithic consensus. And we have come into an electronic dark age, in which the new pagan hordes, with all the power of technology at their command, are on the verge of obliterating the last strongholds of civilized humanity. A vision of death lies before us. As we leave the shores of Christian western man behind, only a dark and turbulent sea of despair stretches endlessly ahead . . . unless we *fight!*

7 / Sexual Mores, the Family, and the Myth of Neutrality

At 5:30 A.M. the sky grows pink just above the blanket of mist at the horizon. The early morning light steals its way into my bedroom. Lying next to me, his fuzzy head on the pillow, is my one-year-old son. His deep, luminous brown eyes stare into mine, as he drinks his bottle of warm milk. I smell his sweet, pale skin, as I nestle my head next to his.

The red rays of sunrise outline his head, adorning it with a rim of light, an orange halo. He finishes his bottle. He places his soft, little hand on my cheek and pats it, looking and waiting to see what I'll do. Ah! What incredibly tender little creatures babies are, reflecting ten times whatever love they are given.

My wife of eleven years of love stirs, opens her gray-green eyes, turns over and looks at me from the other side of his perfect little face.

Suddenly he's up on all fours, crawling around the bed; then he nuzzles his head against my ear, ready to play.

Half an hour later, after his screams of laughter have died away, the baby and I lie exhausted on the bed. He's beginning to doze on my shoulder, his body half-curled, scrunched down on my chest. I could lie here all day.

This is the world God made. This is Christianity. This is love, life and beauty, and fulfillment.

Outside, in the gray misty morning, a generation of people is running off to work, hoping to make as much money as possible. A few of them still know what it's all about, and have left their warm, loving homes reluctantly; necessity compels them to shoulder their responsibilities.

Others, believing their family relationships are of secondary importance, go off to worship themselves at the shrine of their jobs. They do not believe that fulfillment can be found in the joyful little bundle of life that I have in my arms at that moment—family life is too "confining." They prefer the speed and efficiency of a computer console, and bask in its cathode-ray-tube aura. Career, money: these are ultimate values; home, children, and family life, quite secondary. In accepting the prevailing myths of their time, those of self-fulfillment, self-assertion, self-actualization, they have become foolish; for they have thrown away the real earthly treasures, love found within the family.

Work can, and should be, immensely satisfying when it serves the higher goal of supporting one's loved ones and oneself. But work-for-money's-sake, pure materialism, is sterile, a veiled suicide wish.

The Nazis had erected over the gates of the Auschwitz concentration camp the slogan, in two-foot-high letters: "Work makes you free." What they had in mind was not the freedom of family life and love, of course; the "freedom" they sought was their own freedom via the human slave labor they brought into the camp in cattle cars. In much the same way, if not with the same cruelty, those who benefit the most from the arduous labor demanded of people in contemporary societies have with increasing success advertised career as the ultimate value. The powers that be, whether in totalitarian or capitalist nations, have adopted a philosophy in which power through career is the supreme value; they have persuaded us to be of the same mind.

The true God-given rights of men and women have been replaced by man-made, materialistic "rights." The beauty of family life, its warmth, compassion and strength, which have been taken for granted by the myriad generations until most recently, has been replaced by the cold, sterile, bankrupt, selfish "rights" of so-called choice and "liberation." But liberation from what? In the end it turns out that what we are to be liberated from is being fully human.

In American society and the western world, the ascendency of power as the reigning value came about through the destruction of the Judeo-Christian tradition that, while upholding the validity of authority and its right to exercise power, also circumscribed the limits of authority and its use of power. Daniel Henninger, writing in the *Wall Street Journal,* June 30, 1981, discussed the counterculture of the 1960s in relation to the impending television boycott by religious groups and the resurgence of traditional thinking the boycott represented.

> But the idea, implicit in those years, that America could dismantle a 200-year-long tradition of Judeo-Christian morality, a *system* of morality, and substitute for that system a kind of formless, individually derived benevolence, a morality based on feelings and attitudes, was predictably doomed.

Even so, the culture pursued this course, because:

> . . . over some 15 years, the elite groups who set the tone of a nation's moral culture inside its schools, newspapers, magazines, advertisements, TV programs and so forth convinced themselves that they were replacing an unhealthy, constricting system of moral Puritanism with a more humane, enriching system of non-judgmental ethics.
>
> They tried to build a system that asked the rest of the country not to get upset, to remain calm and above all *tolerant* of just about anything any person or group proposed, no matter how tawdry or crackpot it may have been.

An expression of this "formless, individually derived benevolence" to which we were to remain tolerant, the "People's Park" in Berkeley, California remains today as a reminder of humanistic Utopian notions and their effects.

In the spring of 1969, the "street people" claimed that, with "a little help from my friends"—mind-expanding drugs that is—and free speech and free love all would be right with the world. They took over a three-acre patch of land owned by the University of California, not far from the Berkeley campus. Berkeley officials had planned to use the site for a soccer field and student housing, but the street people decided to plant trees, flowers, vegetable gardens, and construct fish ponds and playgrounds instead. They called the spot the "People's Park."

In the dispute over the property with the school, riots ensued and the People's Park became a battleground with National Guardsmen and the police called in to protect the interests of the university. In the aftermath of the violence (in which scores were injured and there was one death), the "people" won. The park became theirs to do with as they pleased. Presumably they would hold one continuous "love-in" and show the rest of the world how life should be lived.

But a visit to the park today will show exactly what the great liberal, humanistic Utopian tradition inevitably produces. The weed-choked lawn is littered with garbage, broken glass, and torn-up asphalt. Winos, drug-addicts, and drifters add to the litter with vomit and excrement, so that getting to the one or two signs of the vegetable patches that were to "feed the people" entails running an obstacle course of debris. The park is a mecca for transients with no place else to go, a fitting symbol of a world view that finally renders all activity meaningless.

The young people of the sixties have become the parents of the eighties. The lack of purpose and confidence found today in the People's Park have extended into family life. Many parents today have little idea what their relationship with their children should be like. The children, of course, have even less of an idea how to love their parents, since, thanks to the new liberal "ethics," the divorce rate and child abuse have skyrocketed. Even in families in which both parents are present, young children are often dumped in day-care centers, while both their parents work ever longer days, frantically trying to stay one step ahead of their credit card interest payments.

I am *not* saying that women necessarily belong at home and men at work. I am saying that both men and women belong at home, in the sense of caring for their children and each other as their chief human priority. Our careers and personal ambitions must always be subservient to the needs of the family. Of course we must work, but it is a question of priorities and daring to sacrifice in a selfish age. Moreover, such sacrifice brings rewards unknown to mere "career fulfillment."

The disintegration of the American family can hardly be stopped by adhering to the "formless benevolence" which has reigned with such destructive results in the past twenty years. But our culture, forgetting its past humanistic failures, refuses to turn aside from its disastrous course. The American family today is headed by men and women who sense the devastation their secularism will produce in their children's lives; but in a culture which continues to scorn the Judeo-Christian tradition, they can only try to "adopt their own values," as our existentialist society recommends. Once again, Daniel Henninger, in his *Wall Street Journal* article, speaks to the peculiar position in which parents today find themselves:

> A woman we know, the mother of three small girls, was saying recently that she and her husband had stopped attending church years ago, though she's always known that if life crunched down on her she could always fall back

on this resource the way a lot of latently religious people do. But it's been bothering her lately that her oldest daughter is entering school and has never even heard of God. For centuries people had the option of rejecting the religion of their childhood, but now that she's part of the first generation to bring up religiously neutered kids, she is beginning to suspect it may not be such a good idea.

Perhaps we might think that this woman could rectify this situation by simply returning to the church with her daughters in tow. Of course, in a way this is true. But the real point is that most such parents, even in a situation of intense anxiety, will not return to the church for fear of "imposing" an "oppressive" morality on their children, and teaching them religious values out of step with today's triumphant and supremely arrogant secularism.

Schools today, having purged themselves of group prayer and other public acknowledgments of God, have tried to find new ways to teach morality. The strategies they have adopted show in their pathetic inadequacy the pompous foolishness of secularism.[1] Terry Eastland, in an article entitled "Teaching Morality in the Public Schools," reports on "moral education" in schools at this time.

> Common to the various "moral education" approaches today is the idea that there is nothing right or wrong and that to teach any substantive ethical precept or idea is to "indoctrinate" students. In one approach, students are invited to "clarify" their own values; the focus is on "rationality," "creativity," "autonomy" and "process." In another approach, students are asked to dwell on ethical dilemmas such as when lying can be justified, or on public policy questions such as the morality of racial quotas.
>
> The problem with these approaches is obvious to anyone raised in the basic morality. In the values approach, no one need fear a teacher's judgment if his values are wrong, because there are no wrong values (other than, of course,

the value of opposing "values" education). Upon learning that all choices are equally valid, a student will be educated into skepticism about morality, fertile soil for wrong action.[2]

Like the mother who knew she always had her traditional religion to fall back on, "values" education might make some sense in the context of the Judeo-Christian tradition. But since our children today are "religiously neutered," what can they possibly make of the proposal that there are hard ethical choices: *the very idea that morality exists is foreign to them*. Mr. Eastland argues, along the lines of J. S. Mill, that whatever the truth of the Judeo-Christian tradition, it should be taught because of its good effect on public behavior: "We have yet to cultivate in this country, at least on a broad scale, a means of teaching the Judeo-Christian ethic without also frequently bringing up its religious roots." That's because, Mr. Eastland, Judeo-Christian morality lives or dies on one's answer to the primary question: *whether Christianity is true*. The courts have decided that the claims of Christianity cannot be discussed in a public educational institution: it had exempted the question; therefore, the good intentions of the Terry Eastlands, the recognition that basic morality must be taught, will go unfulfilled as long as parents cooperate with a "religiously neutered" school system, and as long as the courts foolishly insist on the present course of eliminating any mention of God in public institutions.

We may speculate that the failure of the public educational system to teach growing numbers of students how to read and write may in fact be due to its amoral attitudes. If all values are chosen, none inherent in creation, then why should a student bother to work hard at his studies? What's the point? Why not remain an illiterate zombie munching junk food in front of the television? And even the most obdurate secularist must see some connection between his "value-free" educational system and the incidence of crime, vandalism, and juvenile delinquency that under humanistic liberal tutelage has grown into a virtual state of war.

Higher education has also not been exempt. Harold Fickett writes, "Even the great universities in this country no longer have a comprehensive concept of what an educated man should know. The difficulties Harvard and other universities have encountered in prescribing what courses, apart from the student's departmental specialty or major, will be required for graduation testifies not only to the 'knowledge explosion,' but also to the loss of a common vision. Born of the desire to explore God's world and train young men for his service, Harvard and Yale and the other great private universities have used their heritage of free academic inquiry to profess agnosticism, atheism, and nihilism, and so vitiate their *raison d'etre*."[3]

Nowhere has the schizophrenic double standard of trying to impose absolutely the idea that there are no absolutes borne more bitter fruit than in the confusion husbands and wives experience because of the attack on the traditional family structure. The feminist movement has taken an important role in the breakdown of western civilization's understanding of the family and life itself, running like so many lemmings toward its own destruction.

The book by Betty Friedan, *The Second Stage,* shows by contrast how far the feminist line of thinking has taken us. In the October 12, 1981 issue of *Time* magazine, the writer of a profile of Friedan and her book reports that Friedan "has noted feelings of pain and puzzlement among younger liberated women who set off bravely, launched a career and then discovered that often people are not fulfilled by jobs alone." Friedan believes that feminists—and the *Time* writer acknowledges that many who hold these views are in the feminist mainstream—who belittle the family are out of step with the times. In her new book, Friedan states:

> Virtually all women today share a basic core of commitment to the family and to their own equality within and beyond it, as long as the family and equality are not seen to be in conflict. . . . The choice to have children is a major choice for women not easily denied.

The *Time* writer reports on Friedan's discoveries with a great deal of sympathy and respect. We are implicitly told to take these new views of Friedan's with the utmost seriousness. But look at what Friedan is saying; *she's simply repeating what any grandmother could have told you from the 1950s back to the beginning of time in every single culture.* Friedan has discovered the wheel and *Time* wants us to sit up and take notice! Also, the evident need not to retract her former position, as enunciated in *The Feminine Mystique,* leads Friedan to insist that the family is only an appropriate living arrangement as long as "the family and [a woman's personal] equality are not seen to be in conflict." We've all grown up in families and we all know that each member's "equality" resides only in *belonging.* Any woman—or man, for that matter—who is going to analyze whether his baby's two A.M. feeding impinges on his "equality" simply isn't going to remain in the family for long. Families, like the whole human race, work only through self-sacrifice, not chauvinistic self-fulfillment.

More and more people are recognizing this, but they are not dispensing with the egocentric myths of our time. For some reason a return to the wisdom of the ages and an admission of the failure of the prevailing standards are impossibilities. Never. On no account. Press on. More experimentation, more destruction, more belittling of human worth. If we have failed, let us not blame ourselves!

Society is turning now to its only way out: death. If one merely wants to escape one's problems, committing suicide is a logical conclusion. In a slow and torturous way, that is what our culture is doing in its disregard of family relationships, family structure, authority within that structure, and the desire for children and the parents' commitment to care for their children, and teach them absolutes by which to live.

Obviously, many children are simply being exterminated through abortion. But also the idea of a couple's having children, the source of so much joy to the entire human race, is now *out of fashion*.[4] In the *Wall Street Journal*, on February 1, 1982, a story appeared entitled "Urban Uplift: Youthful Professionals Without Any Children Transform City Areas." The article detailed how a neighborhood in New York City's upper west side, which used to be full of "flophouses" for derelicts, has undergone "gentrification." Old hotels have been made into condominiums which fetch exceedingly high prices. Shops have moved into the neighborhood which cater to the new residents' tastes.

Who are these people willing to pay exorbitant prices to live in a former slum area? They are the young professionals, childless couples who intend to stay that way. The article points out that between 1970 and 1980 the number of couples with no children climbed 23 percent. And the number of unmarried couples "also tripled in the last decade, to almost 1.6 million in 1980." As a result, urban neighborhoods undergoing "gentrification," or a boom in condominiums and shops for young adults, are appearing in many major American cities. The attitudes of John Williams, a recently married thirty-six-year-old, are typical and, to my mind, probably account for the gentrification trend. Williams said, "I knew I couldn't rent an apartment and have a family at the same time. Kids are too expensive, and I guess I'd have to want them a lot to make the sacrifice." That's the contemporary attitude in a nutshell: men and women sacrificing the joy of children to pay exorbitant prices in order to live in a former slum. We live in a time, it seems, in which man, already fallen, will not be satisfied until he has obliterated any trace of the image in which he was made.

The prophet Isaiah, speaking of Israel in rebellion against God, depicts a state of affairs much like our own:

> Ah, sinful nation, a people loaded with guilt, a brood of evil doers, children given to corruption. They have forsaken the Lord; they have spurned the Holy One of Israel and turned their backs on Him.
>
> Why should you be beaten any more? Why do you persist in rebellion? Your whole head is injured, your whole heart afflicted. From the sole of your foot to the top of your head there is no soundness—only wounds and welts and open sores, . . .
>
> When you spread out your hands in prayer, I will hide my eyes from you; even if you offer many prayers, I will not listen. Your hands are full of blood; wash and make yourselves clean. Take your evil deeds out of my sight! Stop doing wrong, learn to do right! Seek justice, encourage the oppressed. Defend the cause of the fatherless, . . .
>
> See how the faithful city has become a harlot! She once was full of justice; righteousness used to dwell in her—but now murderers! . . .
>
> Your rulers are rebels, companions of thieves; they all love bribes and chase after gifts. They do not defend the cause of the fatherless; the widow's case does not come before them. . . .
>
> Their land is full of idols; they bow down to the work of their hands, to what their fingers have made. So men will be brought low and people humbled—but do not forgive them. . . .
>
> Stop trusting in man, who has but breath in his nostrils. Of what account is he? . . .

People will oppress each other—man against man, neighbor against neighbor. The young will rise up against the old, the base against the honorable. . . .

The look on their faces testifies against them; they parade their sin like Sodom; they do not hide it. Woe to them. They have brought disaster upon themselves. . . .

Woe to the wicked! Disaster is upon them! They will be paid back for what their hands have done. Youths oppress my people, women rule over them. Oh my people, your guides lead you astray; they turn you from the path. . . .

Woe to you who add house to house and join field to field till no space is left and you live alone in the land. . . .

They have no regard for the deeds of the Lord, no respect for the work of his hands. . . .

Therefore the grave enlarges its appetite and opens its mouth without limit; . . .

Woe to those who bind with cords of deceit, . . .

Woe to those who call evil good and good evil, who put darkness for light and light for darkness, who put bitter for sweet and sweet for bitter.

Woe to those who are wise in their own eyes and clever in their own sight. . . .

If one looks at the land, he will see darkness and distress; even the light will be darkened by the clouds. . . .

The ever hearing, but never understanding; the ever seeing, but never perceiving.[5]

History repeats itself; Isaiah's account of his times sounds very familiar, doesn't it? Deceit, duplicity, double standards, unrighteousness, the committing of abominations, the roles of the sexes reversed: what could be a more accurate description of our own day and age? Our humanistic society has fallen in love with sterility and ugliness and death. It calls good evil and evil good. Orwell's *1984* contains little, if anything, that we cannot find in our world today or see as imminent.

In C. S. Lewis's magnificent *Chronicles of Narnia,* in the volume called *The Silver Chair,* we read about a brave band deep underground effecting the rescue of a prince. The wicked sorceress, who is actually a snake, has turned herself into a beautiful and charming woman. After she has surreptitiously thrown a stupefying magic powder onto the fire, she strums, strums, strums on her mandolin. The band, in order to rescue the prince, should attack her, but the music, the comfortable warmth of the room and the sweet, heavy smell of the magic powder begin to put them to sleep or into a dazed, hypnotic state.

Fortunately, one of the band, Puddleglum, has the presence of mind to stamp out the fire so that the magic powder ceases to rule their wits.

To me the story captures in allegory the situation in which those of Judeo-Christian principle find ourselves. The media often like to portray the moral disintegration of our nation in fatalistic terms that diminishes resistance. "Since abortion is inevitable," they ask, "why not legalize it?" In this way they strum their mandolins and cast their numbing powders into the fire; we feel helpless, caught up in a predetermined course of hopeless events which, despite our actions, cannot be changed.

Often those who believe in the Lord fall prey to this kind of thinking. We see it in Jonah running away from Nineveh. He had not taken into account, truly believed, that if he obeyed God's command and voiced God's message in his time, the prevailing attitudes in Nineveh could change. We must learn the lesson of Jonah. No matter how unequivocally the media and academic community condemn our efforts, we must be faithful to the Lord's command and to true, humane Christian values. We must not accept the "inevitability arguments" of the opposition.

Richard John Neuhaus, writing a statement of purpose for the newly formed Institute on Religion and

Democracy of Washington, D.C., addressed the fatalism of our times and the Christians' appropriate response:

> The apology for oppression declares that liberal democracy is decadent and dying. It claims that we should welcome, or at least resign ourselves to, inevitable revolutionary change under totalitarian auspices. *We declare, however, that history is not the sphere of the inevitable but the sphere of freedom* [my emphasis].
>
> Within the limits of a life that is bounded by death, free men and women strive for what should be; they do not surrender to what others say must be.[6]

To reinforce this point, we should remember that the ruling class of the British Empire used to speak of the inevitability of its power. I'm sure King George believed that those primitive bumpkins in the American colonies were certainly in no position to throw off the yoke of Great Britain. But his perspective was limited.

The French royal family used to dismiss the idea that there could be a revolution, by saying, in effect, "Well, they're only peasants and we are of royal blood." Their perspective was limited; events turned out differently.

In our own day, attempts by Christians to speak out are dismissed also. Daniel Henninger in the aforementioned *Wall Street Journal* article articulates the unspoken fears of the liberal humanist elite, which he calls sarcastically the "Voices of Reason." They, he says, "are afraid in great part that, given an opening, these morally strait-laced groups will refashion American society in the image of Southern Baptists (the Southerners are actually the most effectively scary stand-in for whatever smacks of small towns, Midwestern suburbs, or anything west of the Hudson River and east of Los Angeles)." But we must not be put off with these cries of "the peasants are coming, the peasants are coming!" We will not let the powers-that-be shirk the questions the "peasants" are raising. That many who speak out may wear ill-fitting polyester suits and the wrong kind of shoes has nothing whatsoever to do with the truth of their message, and we must not let our superficial critics evade the issues. Nor must we let the self-serving, compromising evangelical leadership get away with passing by on the other side of those who dare, in an effort to save their "respectability," to change the course of events.

In an important way, history is not open-ended: God directs it. Our choices do make a difference, however, and our actions are among the means God uses. We cannot merely say, "Well, it's in God's hands," and feel we have done our job. The Old Testament prophets did not respond to the unrighteousness of their time in this manner. Neither did Christ, and we are called to be his body, the extension of his being, in the world. Christians cannot be fatalists, transfixed by their own ideas of "predestination" or by the secularist version of this concept, "inevitability." Of all people, Christians should not be the friend of the status quo, for the status quo, the reign of the devil, is what Christ came to redeem. To speak of a gospel that does not have political implications or a Bible whose laws do not apply to the modern world subverts the entire thrust of Christianity, which is to reclaim for God what has been lost through man's disobedience. To accept the idea that there is any part of life that Christianity should not affect, whether it be the family, politics, the law, the media, or the arts, is to make a tacit admission that Christianity is not true.

We must act, and act now. We must dare to be human. We must dare to sacrifice in a selfish age. We must dare to be unfashionable. Dare to live, and dare to let the defenseless live.

8 / A Time for Anger in the Arts

Some time ago, I wrote a book called *Addicted to Mediocrity*. That book pointed out the lack of participation by Christians, especially evangelicals, in the arts and media. I concentrated there primarily on the reasons within the Christian community for this being so.

But while most conservative Protestants or evangelicals have neglected the arts, a few heroic individuals have exercised their God-given talents. Indeed, despite the trend toward skepticism in culture as a whole, great Christian artists have appeared in our time in numbers that the secular world finds troubling.[1]

Because the secular world has determined that Christianity is not only untrue but an archaic world view which must be eradicated, it increasingly applies a double standard to art produced by Christians. The myth of neutrality holds sway in the arts, as it does in politics and the law. This must be attacked and exposed for the bigotry and provincial narrow-mindedness that it is, if art made by Christians is to play its important role in redemption.

To cite an example of anti-Christian bigotry in this area, think of the books, both nonfiction and fiction, which appear on the best seller lists. The *New York Times'* best seller list, as well as *Time* magazine's best seller list, contribute without a doubt to the sale and popularity of the works on the list; when a title appears it immediately enjoys a boost in sales and comes to the attention of an enormous public that otherwise might not hear of it.

The lists, therefore, make a substantial difference in the number of copies of a book that are eventually sold.

Beyond commercial success, books that appear on these lists attract more attention from the rest of the media in terms of reviews and follow-up stories; the book's content thus enjoys a full public discussion: its ideas help shape our culture.

A typical nonfiction work on the *New York Times'* best seller list has sold between 60,000 and 120,000 copies; works of fiction can qualify with fewer sales. Books by Christians published by Christian book companies, however, both nonfiction and fiction titles, almost never appear on these lists *even though many Christian books in any given year sell far in excess of the number of copies which qualify a book to appear on the lists.*

The reason that books by Christians rarely appear on the best seller lists, even though they outsell their contemporary secular counterparts, often by a ratio of 3 to 1, is simple: the secular world is provincial, narrow-minded and bigoted.[2]

It has often been said of New Yorkers that their world ends at the Hudson River. Certainly this provincial mentality characterizes such corporations as Time, Inc. and the *New York Times* when it comes to assessing the fiction and nonfiction books by authors within the Christian community. This bigotry even extends to reviews. As Harold Fickett says, "The kind of begrudging reviews a fine novelist like Frederick Buechner often receives testify that in the main those who run the publishing world are annoyed that they are obliged even to discuss Christianity."[3]

Imagine what would happen if a racial minority group could show that the works of its authors were being deliberately discriminated against—the denunciations, the accusations of McCarthyism, the vitriolic columns and stinging orations that would ensue. But the ever-silent Christian community has yet to protest in any significant way about the systematic neglect of Christian books, and so we do not even take advantage of those who truly believe in free speech, who might be our allies.

The news and publishing empires excuse their bigotry by saying that they take their count from "mainline secular bookstores" and that "religious books" are in another category since they are sold mostly out of Christian bookstores. This simply will not wash. If one looks at the best seller lists at any given time, there are many books with highly religious and philosophical implications; in fact, it's impossible to write a serious book on almost any topic without its having a directly religious significance. But those works which appear on the best seller lists generally espouse secular humanism, and so they are "neutral." It's the same old story. And the defense of the lists on the basis that religious books are in another category fails because cook books, sex manuals, and game books appear regularly; the idea of these lists being specialized rather than general is specious. All books fall into categories, and to rule out religious books is pure arbitrary bigotry. Not to bother to include counts of books sold through religious bookstores is self-serving laziness.

If the best seller lists were really what they claim to be, books by Christians would show up with startling frequency; their sales figures would put them at the top of these lists regularly. And this would impress the general public that Christians might actually have something to say and would make it necessary for those in the media to take Christianity seriously.

This, however, is what an organization such as the *New York Times,* which represents itself as a champion of "pluralism," wants to avoid like the plague. They deliberately promote the idea of a de-spiritualized, secular world, at the same time continuing to claim their best seller lists are accurate!

It surprises me that no legal action has been taken by the Christian Booksellers' Association, or individual

Christian bookstores, or Christian authors, or publishing companies, or legal associations against these practices. Open discrimination exists, and we ought to demand reparations for the financial losses which have resulted as a way of challenging this secularist bigotry.

The lack of integrity in the case of best seller lists is not unique. The absence of coverage of Christian events and personalities is another example.[4] Christians who work in any branch of the arts face the open discrimination of liberal zealots. In fact, we live in an era in which liberals, for all their professed horror at the foolish and wrong-headed conservatives who take the novels of a fine author like Kurt Vonnegut off library shelves, censor and suppress books with views contrary to their own with more subtle and effective methods.[5]

Conservative Protestants, Catholics, and other religious people at times have tried to limit books available in schools and so forth, and have been condemned as "censors." However, the liberal media take a different view of liberal innovations in the area of censorship. *Newsweek* (March 29, 1982), in an article entitled "Women Pioneers Find Their Pulpits," quotes a Ms. Priesand, the first woman rabbi in New Jersey, as wishing to change what she considers the sexist language of the liturgy (mankind, our fathers, God our Father). "I want customs and ceremonies to be equal for everyone," she says. "That will make religion more accessible to women."

While conservatives may attempt to limit the use of books in schools, they have never gone so far as trying to pretend they have never existed at all.

The liberal book burner, not satisfied with merely limiting what is accessible to himself, herself, his children, or whomever, wishes to actually rewrite history and eliminate words and paragraphs from the English language forever, and totally. Imagine the outcry from the Jewish community should a Jerry Falwell say he wished to "Protestantize" the Torah or the outcry from the liberal media if some conservative evangelical leader announced that he wished to rewrite portions of black history or change their language to make them more accessible to whites and less "African."

But in the *Newsweek* article, such a statement, when dealing with the basic tenets of Judaism, passes without comment; in fact, the slant of the article is favorable toward such "innovations."

Another example of the book-burning mentality of the liberal humanist today is the zealous drive by the feminist movement to recreate the next generation in its own image. The feminist attempt to manipulate the educational process has been extremely successful. Feminists have so pressured and lobbied the textbook publishers into cowering acquiescence that there are almost no exceptions to the rule when it comes to giving textbooks the slant they desire. Michael Levin, a professor of philosophy at City College of New York writing in *Commentary* magazine, June 1982, says,

> When parents object to profanity in school books, they are invariably met wih answering cries of "censorship" or "thought control," and warned of the dangers of tampering with the First Amendment. Yet, while national attention has been focused on the activities of such concerned individuals, one of the most extensive thought control campaigns in American educational history has gone completely ignored. I am referring to the transformation, in the name of "sex fairness," of textbooks and curricula at all educational levels, with the aim of convincing children that boys and girls are the same. Indeed, a dismantling of "sex roles" has virtually superseded transmission of information as the aim of the classroom.

Michael Levin then goes on to quote the feminist instructions imposed on the textbook writers for the various major textbook publishers such as Macmillan, Scott Foresman, Harper & Row, etc. For instance, at Southwestern Publishing, the instructions read: "Emphasis is on what can be and should be, rather than mirroring what the society is in terms of sex roles." The feminists have imposed a rigorous liturgy and ideology on the whole educational system, even though they *do not represent the majority opinion in many parts of society*.

Once again this is a classic example of the myth of neutrality. The Christian, the fundamentalist, the evangelical, the Orthodox, the Catholic, and the Jew are meant to sit silently and not interpose their religious beliefs on society, particularly when it comes to education. And yet, within one generation an extreme feminist and humanist ideology in educational textbooks has supplanted the traditional Judeo-Christian view. The extremes to which these new textbook writers will go to impose their ideology is emphasized by Michael Levin when he points out that traditional roles for women such as mother, wife, and homemaker are almost never portrayed in the new textbooks as something that could even be considered! Once again, supposed liberals have been more interested in stamping out all other points of view and options than successfully arguing their own case.

The censorship of neglect functions in films as well. Upon completion of *Whatever Happened to the Human Race?*, our company approached various television stations and networks, including PBS, about airing a ninety-minute version of the film. Since the abortion issue at the time was very "hot," and since public television had programmed a considerable amount of material on the pro-abortion side, we naively felt we stood a good chance of presenting the other side of the argument, reflecting the prolife view held by many Americans. And since Americans' tax dollars were paying for much of the programming through government grants, we could claim our right to be heard. In addition, the quality of the film being excellent (even Judy Mann in *The Washington Post* granted us that, albeit in a left-handed manner), we prevented the all too often legitimate excuse, when secularists try to ignore Christian programs, of technical shoddiness.

One of our associates took the films and tried to get an appointment with PBS in Washington, D.C. The network refused to program the film on the basis that it could not possibly air something of so "one-sided" a nature. This, of course, did not come as a complete shock, but it did confirm once again how the zealous liberal humanist fails to follow through with his belief in free speech.

Later, we found out that at the same time PBS was turning down our show, they were preparing the series called *Hard Choices,* which those who have read thus far know must be the most outspoken proabortion, proinfanticide, and proeuthanasia program ever put forward. *Hard Choices* brought us the "unbiased" views in its magazine companion of Messieurs Provine, Dworkin, and Joseph Fletcher. If that's not hypocrisy, nothing is. But similar decisions are made daily.

In this so-called land of opportunity, one is led to expect that the master of an art form will have his chance to be heard. This is true for just about any group in our society, including the lunatic fringes, it would seem, except for those who express traditional Judeo-Christian teaching within their work. One would fare far better attempting to promote a film depicting the joys, let us say, of homosexual incest as a "fulfilling lifestyle" than one arguing for Christian truth, or something as unfashionable as the sanctity of all life.

From TV sitcoms to the rarefied atmosphere of New York Art Galleries, the secular humanist expresses his point of view with increasing stridency. No one ever attempts to provide a forum for the Christian artistic reply. The artistic community at large holds the same position as the Unitarian and Universalist churches; that is, *it's OK to believe anything and do just about anything you want as long as you don't believe in traditional Judeo-Christian teachings and ethics or do something so absolutely outrageous as to take the teachings of the Bible seriously, let alone literally.*

There are, of course, exceptions but their appearance occurs so infrequently that they do nothing more than draw attention to the rule. (*Chariots of Fire* comes to mind as a case in point. When was the last time you saw a missionary portrayed as a hero?)[6] While Christians have failed to contribute to the arts as much as they should have in recent years, there are again far more talented Christian writers, artists, filmmakers, dancers, and musicians than there would appear to be from the slim recognition they are given by a secularist, pagan, provincial elite.

In my own career I well remember the time when I was in Hollywood talking with Stephen Bach, who at that time was senior vice-president in charge of worldwide productions for United Artists. Through a series of events, he had seen part of my film *Whatever Happened to the Human Race?* He liked the film well enough to talk with me about making a feature film for United Artists.

In the course of that discussion, he told me in so many words that I was fortunate he was open-minded, as most people in town (Hollywood) wouldn't have allowed me inside the office if they thought I actually might hold the views espoused in our films. He then went on to ask me whether I "personally held" these views or whether it was "just a job." When I told him the film expressed my views, he was rather dismayed. Reflecting on the matter afterwards, I couldn't imagine such a question being posed had I come in after making a typically humanistic, liberal statement about "rational suicide" or another aspect of our brave new world.[7]

The liberal humanist often pretends in his art to be making "radical statements" and delivering society from the "old taboos." (Talk about whipping a dead horse!) In fact, he just mirrors the prevailing consensus, his views, strangely enough, having been accepted by the establishment. Therefore, liberal humanistic art today, under the mantle of radicalism, is in fact the establishment. *The Christian in the arts is the true revolutionary and outsider. He does not represent the old order (long since destroyed), but a new departure.*

Negative labels are often put on Christian artistic efforts. For instance, when the *New York Times* reviewed our film and seminar *Whatever Happened to the Human Race?* the headline was, "Fundamentalists Hold Pro-life Seminar." What other group has their religious convictions mentioned? Can you imagine a headline that starts, "liberal secular humanists gather at Planned Parenthood rally on world population control"?

Christians who wish to break into the arts do so at their own peril. We have no choice in the matter, however. The arts, as other cultural endeavors, *must be reclaimed* by those with something more humane to say than the destructive, antireligious secularist message. The work of a hundred years of humanistic artistic endeavor, which has contributed so markedly to moving society away from the compassionate principles of Judeo-Christian truth toward the dark, negative hopelessness of the end of the twentieth century, must be countered. We must hold the liberal to his word. If he wants to have his "pluralistic society," very well, but as part of that culture, let us demand that our voice be heard.

Ironically, the secularist art world cannot live by its standards. By and large, it ignores present-day Christian artistic contributions; nevertheless, it finds its own artistic productions devoid of substance and turns to the past for nourishment.

Imagine a world in which all the music composed before the twentieth century would not be played.

Imagine a world in which all pre-twentieth century paint-ing and sculpture would not exist. Imagine a world in which all literary texts before 1908 would be suppressed.

Of western man's great achievements in the arts only the Greek and Roman classics and some of the works of the Enlightenment would be left if we ruled out the crea-tions of those who either were personally Christian, or at least lived within the Judeo-Christian framework, accept-ing it as a matter of course. For example, Shakespeare can hardly be considered a fundamentalist, but more signifi-cantly the moral vision of his plays depends utterly on Christianity.

One cannot listen only to *musique concrète,* punk rock, or atonal noise: Bach is played now more than ever. Jack-son Pollock and deKooning must at some point be relieved by the eye's pleasure in the natural forms of Gothic archi-tecture, the light in a Vermeer, and the feeling for weight, mass, and power in the work of Michelangelo. The hope-lessness of Beckett's trashcan characters must at some point be exchanged for the joy of the lovers in "A Mid-Summer Night's Dream."

In other words, the proud secular humanist cannot live in the world he has created and remain sane without drawing on the Judeo-Christian artistic heritage. This alone should make him rethink his position. Why the need for music, artworks, literature, and other cultural artifacts that in terms of his own philosophical position are absurd? If he is right, why does he still need these things? Because, whoever the hu-manist believes man to be, man is who he is: a being created in God's image. His longing for beauty, resolu-tion, order, and transformation cannot simply be canceled by philosophical fiat!

Yet, no one addresses the glaring inconsistency of the person who rejects Christian truth today, while depending on all the benefits of what it has produced in the arts (or law and government) before his own time. Once again, where are the Christians howling with rage? Or, like Elijah, why don't we ridicule those who believe in gods that cannot consume their sacrifices with holy fire?

There is nothing more profane than the image of an atheist with tears in his eyes conducting the glory and passion of Handel's *Messiah*. This image, and others like it, which we encounter everywhere, denies the historical fact that Handel's music *would not have been possible without the religious inspiration behind it.*

One imagines, on the day of judgment, such a man standing before Almighty God and not being condemned on biblical grounds at all but simply on the basis of his own self-contradictions, his hypocrisy.

It is not as though the artwork of Christians through the centuries does not provide a clear testimony. C. S. Lewis came to Christianity partially through confronting the division between his aesthetic and moral life. He began to wonder why, while he rejected all things Christian, his favorite literary figures from Milton onwards were believers, and at the same time those with whom he tended to agree philosophically produced literature he could not bear. He had the guts and open-mindedness and the true liberality to pursue such a line of thought and inquiry. This led him inevitably to Christianity. Unhappily, most figures in the arts today do not have such an open mind. The example of Lewis shows how few take the path right before them to ultimate truth.

I have a vision of someone like Hugh Hefner sitting in his company mansion, penning a diatribe against "repressive" Christian morality, while Gregorian chant plays on his quadrophonic stereo system in the background.

I see an atheistic professor of sociology on holiday in France, eating his picnic lunch in the shade of Chartres Cathedral, while he works on the notes of a speech lamenting the conversion to Christianity of some quaint tribe of cannibals.

I hear the sound of a baby aborted in the third trimester, crying feebly as it dies in a blood-stained tray. Its cries are muffled by the melody of "Jesu, Joy of Man's Desiring" playing on the FM station in the abortionist's waiting room.

It is time for those who are Christian to reassert themselves in the arts. And it is time for the Christian community to back them. We must fill people's imaginations with the images of the Christian vision. *The arts and media must be a focal point for protest against the pagan world that has come upon us, while we have had our Christian heads in the sand of "spirituality."*

Fight for a fair hearing. Fight to overcome the secularist bigotry. Fight for life and the right of *all* to live. Fight to give the Christian voice new and positive images. Fight the mentality of compromise and silence exhibited by much of the Christian media.

To my fellow workers in the arts I say, create, strive for excellence, and above all, never be silent!

9 / A Time for Misbehaving

Christians and those of Judeo-Christian principle have been far too well behaved in the recent past.

Every person of true moral principle is on a collision course with the modern, inhuman, technological state and society in which we live. Every person of true moral principle should be prepared to stand and fight against this "brave new world."

The Jews have endured state and often religious persecution throughout history for not abandoning their principles. The early Christians went to the lions rather than transgress God's law and bow to a secular power. *They were rebels; the Romans saw them as having committed acts of civil disobedience.*

Christ himself died rather than compromise. All he had to say to the high priest was that he was not God; or he could have renounced his claim to be a king before the Romans, and he would have gone free.

Atrocities unthinkable a few years ago go on today with the state's sanction. More are in the offing. Why is there such roaring, massive silence on the part of those who should know better? *Abortion, infanticide, euthanasia, and a deliberate assault on the family structure are realities. The continued curbing of religious freedom grinds on. They are a part of our world no matter how long we pretend otherwise.*

Writing in *Commentary* magazine (April 1982), Norman Ravitch speaks of the Christian involvement in society today in the following terms:

Like the proverbial poor Greeks, who survive by taking in one another's wash, theologians and scholars in religious studies write primarily for one another; seldom does the import of their labors have any effect on the consciousness of Christian believers or on the wider educated public.

The silence, noninvolvement, studious "scholarship" and other tactics used by Christians to avoid involving themselves in society around them must stop. Evangelists and theologians who hide behind their "evangelical work" or their theology or, as Ravitch says, their tendency to write in a private language merely for one another, must stop.

We must once again commit ourselves to a robust view of truth. *Religious people must once again become involved in every area of life: politics, law, medicine, family life, education, science, the media, and the arts.* We must provide the example of an alternate way of living by placing our children and their care before our own ambitions and materialism.

Where are our champions?

The ACLU and other elitist, "civil libertarian" absolutists never rest. Christian lawyers have too often been more intent on holding theoretical seminars and "fellowshipping together."

The arrogant attitude of the abortion-rich medical profession grows more and more inhuman day by day. The abortion clinics hack babies apart and burn them to death with saline solutions. Where are the Christian champions of medicine as a vocation, a healing science, one that fights to *save* life?

The so-called pluralistic politician and judge move toward greater and greater control of the citizenry. Where are the Christian men and women to stand up and fight in the political arena *without compromise?*

Many theologians, evangelists, leaders of para-church organizations, local pastors, publishers, and Christian magazines *have cultivated a careful silence on these issues.* In the main, the whole evangelical circus parades before the world, its act declaring the Bible is irrelevant to the activities of government and society. To many so-called evangelical leaders, cultivating acceptance seems to have replaced principle.

Often, when Christian and evangelical leaders have spoken up, it has been on social issues that are conveniently acceptable and fashionable. Nuclear disarmament seems to be something evangelical leaders and some Roman Catholic bishops can easily espouse when they are given a sympathetic media hearing and the support of a mass movement. When it comes to taking up the cause of "Baby Doe," however, or some other such unfortunate, all of a sudden the stage is bare of any leaders who will come and act on behalf of the truly poor. *It seems to be easier to speak of fashionable, theoretical impending doom than to deal with the actual inhuman realities of the humanistic consensus.*

The public educational system turns out generation after generation of baffled, rootless, religiously neutered neo-barbarians, who have been taught that there are no moral absolutes; they have been delivered by that system into the hands of such persons as Planned Parenthood's high priests and instructed in their pitiful religion of "do your own thing."

Where is the Christian counter-attack on these modern-day death camps? Where have we been and what will we do now to save our country and the rest of western civilization from the future that the bio-engineers and power-hungry ethicists have in store? We must choose between a secular Caesar, the bondage and death of an all-powerful state, with the most powerful techniques of control ever known at its disposal, or the God of the Old and New Testaments.

The alternative to standing up and taking action finds expression in the Book of Isaiah, chapter 7, verse 11: "For how long, O Lord? And He answered, until the cities lie ruined and without inhabitants, until the houses are left deserted and fields ruined and ravaged, until the Lord has sent everyone far away and the land is utterly forsaken." A little later, the solution comes: "The Lord Almighty is the one you are to regard as holy, He is the one you are to fear, He is the one you are to dread, and He will be a sanctuary."

We are not to seek the approval of man or fear the ridicule of a short-sighted secularist world. In the end, it is God we must fear and Him we must obey. To obey the bureaucracies, the courts, the whims and social trends of a humanistic culture, even the debates and edicts of co-opted theologians, is to forsake obedience to the One to whom ultimate obedience is due.

In the Book of James, chapter 2, we read:

> What good is it, my brothers, if a man claims to have faith but has no deeds? Can such a faith save him? Suppose a brother or sister is without clothes and daily food. If one of you says to him, "Go, I wish you well; keep warm and well fed," but does nothing about his physical needs, what good is it? In the same way, faith by itself, if it is not accompanied by action, is dead.
>
> But someone will say, you have faith and I have deeds. Show me your faith without deeds, and I will show you my faith by what I do. You believe that there is one God. Good! Even the demons believe that—and shudder.
>
> You foolish men, do you want evidence that faith without deeds is useless?

The evidence in our own day that "faith without deeds is useless" surrounds us everywhere. Having accepted the myth of neutrality, the opposition's lie, we have given over the battlefield to the enemy and they have run rampant.

Ours has been a religion of faith without deeds for too long. It is time that mighty deeds be done again. Truth equals confrontation.

Appendix / Abortion[1]

by Liz Jeffries and Rick Edmonds

A woman's scream broke the late-night quiet and brought two young obstetrical nurses rushing to Room 4456 of the University of Nebraska Medical Center. The patient, admitted for an abortion, had been injected 30 hours earlier with a salt solution, which normally kills the fetus and causes the patient to deliver a mass of lifeless tissue, in a process similar to a miscarriage.

This time, though, something had gone wrong. When nurse Marilyn Wilson flicked on the lights and pulled back the covers, she found, instead of the stillborn fetus she'd expected, a live 2½-pound baby boy, crying and moving his arms and legs there on the bed.

Dismayed, the second nurse, Joanie Fuchs, gathered the squirming infant in loose bedcovers, dashed down the corridor and called to the other nurses for help. She did not take the baby to an intensive care nursery, but deposited it instead on the stainless steel drainboard of a sink in the maternity unit's Dirty Utility Room—a large closet where bedpans are emptied and dirty linens stored. Other nurses and a resident doctor gathered and gaped.

Finally, a head nurse telephoned the patient's physician, Dr. C. J. LaBenz, at home, apparently waking him.

"He told me to leave it where it was," the head nurse testified later, "just to watch it for a few minutes, that it would probably die in a few minutes."

This was in Omaha, in September 1979. It was nothing new. Hundreds of times a year in the United States, an

155

aborted fetus emerges from the womb kicking and alive. Some survive. A baby girl in Florida, rescued by nurses who found her lying in a bedpan, is 5 years old now and doing well. Most die. The Omaha baby lasted barely 2½ hours after he was put in the closet with the dirty linen.

Always, their arrival is met with shock, dismay and confusion.

When such a baby is allowed to die and the incident becomes known, the authorities often try to prosecute the doctor. This has happened several dozen times in the past eight years, most recently in the case of Dr. LaBenz, who is to go on trial in Omaha this fall on two counts of criminal abortion. But interviews with nurses, some of them visibly anguished, uncovered dozens of similar cases that never reached public attention.

In fact, for every case that does become known, a hundred probably go unreported. Dr. Willard Cates, an expert on medical statistics who is chief of abortion surveillance for the Center for Disease Control in Atlanta, estimates that 400 to 500 abortion live births occur every year in the United States. That is only a tiny fraction of the nation's 1.5 million annual abortions. Still, it means that these unintended live births are literally an everyday occurrence.

They are little known because organized medicine, from fear of public clamor and legal action, treats them more as an embarrassment to be hushed up than a problem to be solved. "It's like turning yourself in to the IRS for an audit," Cates said. "What is there to gain? The tendency is not to report because there are only negative incentives."

One result of the medical community's failure to openly acknowledge the problem is that many hospitals and clinics give their staffs no guidelines for dealing with abortion live births. Even where guidelines exist, they may not be followed. The doctor is seldom present when a live birth occurs, because most late abortions—those done later than the midpoint of pregnancy—are performed by the injection of a solution (the method used in the Omaha case) that slowly induces delivery of the fetus many hours later. Crucial decisions therefore fall to nurses and physician residents with secondary authority over the case.

Signs of life in the baby may or may not be recognized. At some hospitals a live-born abortion baby is presumed dead unless it conspicuously demonstrates otherwise, by crying or waving its arms and legs. Even then, the medical personnel on the scene may let the baby die rather than try to save it.

Because they are premature, these infants need immediate care, including machine support, in order to live. Given such care, many can survive in good health, as did a pair of abortion babies in separate incidents in Wilmington, Del., in the spring of 1979 and since adopted. Others are too premature to be saved even with the best care.

Whether they live or die, these abortion live births—and even successful, routine abortions of late term, highly developed fetuses—are taking a heavy emotional toll on medical staffs across the country. Some physicians say they have "burned out" and have stopped doing abortions altogether. Nursing staffs at hospitals in Cleveland, Grand Rapids, Fort Lauderdale and elsewhere have rebelled at late abortions and have stopped their hospitals from performing any abortions later than the midpoint of pregnancy. Some staff members who regularly perform late abortions report having nightmares about fetuses, including recurring dreams in which they frantically seek to hide fetuses from others.

In legalizing abortion in 1973, the Supreme Court said it was reserving the right to protect the life of a viable fetus—that is, one with the potential to survive outside the womb. But the court never directly acknowledged the chance of an aborted fetus' being born alive, and it therefore never gave a clear guideline for dealing with what Dr.

Thomas Kerenyi, a leading New York expert on abortions, has called "the dreaded complication."

Twenty states (including Pennsylvania, New Jersey and Delaware) have no laws limiting late abortions or mandating care for live-born abortion babies. Even where such state laws exist, they are considered by some to be unconstitutional.

"Everyone—doctors, attorneys, state legislators—is looking for some clear guidelines concerning disposition of these infants," said Newman Flanagan, district attorney for the City of Boston. "If a baby has rejected an abortion and lives, then it is a person under the Constitution. As such, it has a basic right to life. Unfortunately, it is difficult to protect that right, because there are no guidelines addressed to this specific issue."

Medical trends indicate that abortion live births will continue. They may even become more frequent. For one thing, demand for late-term abortions is undiminished, and with the growing popularity of genetic testing to screen for fetal defects midway through pregnancy, educated and affluent women are now joining the young, the poor and the uninformed who have been, until now, the main groups seeking late abortions.

Furthermore, estimating the gestational age of a fetus in the womb—a crucial aspect of a successful abortion—remains an inexact art. In March, doctors at the Valley Abortion Clinic in Phoenix estimated that one woman was 19 to 20 weeks pregnant; days later she delivered not an aborted fetus but a 2½-pound, 32-week baby. It survived after two months of intensive care at a Phoenix hospital.

Finally, medical science in the past 10 years has greatly improved its ability to care for premature babies. Infants are becoming viable earlier and earlier. Those with a gestational age of 24 weeks and weighing as little as 1½ pounds can now survive if given the best of care.

So long as doctors perform abortions up to the 24th week of pregnancy (as is legal everywhere in the United States under the 1973 Supreme Court ruling), it is statistically certain that some of these borderline cases will turn out to be viable babies, born alive. It happened again last May in Chicago—a 19-to-20 week estimate, a live-born 2-pound baby boy.

By ignoring the problem of abortion live births, the court and the medical establishment are choosing to overlook a long, well-documented history of cases:

January 1969. Stobhill Hospital, Glasgow, Scotland: A custodian heard a cry from a paper bag in the snow beside an incinerator. He found a live baby. It was taken inside and cared for in the hospital's operating theater but died nine hours later. The infant's gestational age had been estimated at 26 weeks by the physician performing the abortion. It was actually closer to 32 weeks. No efforts were made to check for signs of life before the aborted baby was discarded. No charges were filed. Because the case had been written about in British medical journals, it was a matter of record—before abortion was legalized in this country—that such things could happen.

April 1973. Greater Bakersfield Hospital, Bakersfield, Calif.: A 4½-pound infant was born live following a saline abortion (induced by an injection of salt solution) performed by Dr. Xavier Hall Ramirez. Informed by phone, Dr. Ramirez ordered two nurses to discontinue administering oxygen to the baby. His instructions were countermandated by another doctor; the baby survived and later was placed for adoption. Ramirez was indicted for solicitation to commit murder. His attorney argued that a medical order based on medical opinion, no matter how mistaken, is privileged. Dr. Irvin M. Cushner of the University of California at Los Angeles, later to become a top health policy official in the Carter administration, testified that it was normal for Ramirez to expect the delivery of a dead or certain-to-die infant as the result of a saline abortion.

July 1974. West Penn Hospital, Pittsburgh: Dr. Leonard Laufe performed an abortion on a woman who contended she had been raped—though that and her account of when she became pregnant were later disputed. She had been turned down for an abortion at another hospital, where the term of her pregnancy was estimated at 26 to 31 weeks. Laufe put it at 20 to 22. The abortion, induced by an injection of prostaglandin, a substance that stimulates muscle contraction and delivery of the fetus, was filmed for use as an instructional film. The film showed the three-pound infant moving and gasping. Also, a nurse and a medical student testified that they had noticed signs of life. No charges were filed, however, after a coroner's inquest at which Laufe testified that the infant sustained fatal damage during delivery.

February 1975. Boston: Dr. Kenneth Edelin was convicted of manslaughter for neglecting to give care to a 24-week infant after a 1973 abortion at Boston City Hospital. Witnesses said Edelin held the infant down, constricting the flow of oxygen through the umbilical cord and smothering it. He was the first and only American doctor ever convicted on charges of failing to care for an infant born during an abortion. The conviction was overturned by the Massachusetts Supreme Court on the ground that improper instructions had been given to the jury. Edelin and his lawyer argued that he had taken no steps to care for the infant because it was never alive outside the womb.

March 1977. Westminster Community Hospital, Westminster, Calif.: A seven-month baby girl was born live after a saline abortion performed by Dr. William Waddill. A nurse testified that Waddill, when he got to the hospital, interrupted her efforts to help the baby's breathing. A fellow physician testified that he had seen Waddill choke the infant. "I saw him put his hand on the baby's neck and push down," said Dr. Ronald Cornelson. "He said, 'I can't find the goddamn trachea,' and 'This baby won't stop breathing.' " Two juries, finding Cornelson an emotional and unconvincing witness, deadlocked in two separate trials. Charges against Waddill were then dismissed. He had contended the infant was dying of natural causes by the time he got to the hospital.

July 1979. Cedars-Sinai Medical Center, Los Angeles: Dr. Boyd Cooper delivered an apparently stillborn infant, after having ended a problem pregnancy of 23 weeks. Half an hour later the baby made gasping attempts to breathe, but no efforts were made to resuscitate it because of its size (1 pound 2 ounces) and the wishes of the parents. The baby was taken to a small utility room that was used, among other things, as an infant morgue. Told of the continued gasping, Cooper instructed a nurse, "Leave the baby there—it will die." Twelve hours later, according to testimony of the nurse, Laura VanArsdale, she returned to work and found the infant still in the closet, still gasping.

Cooper then agreed to have the baby boy transferred to an intensive care unit, where he died four days later. A coroner's jury ruled the death "accidental" rather than natural but found nothing in Cooper's conduct to warrant criminal action.

A common thread in all these incidents is that life was recognized and the episode brought to light by someone other than the doctor. Indeed, there is evidence that doctors tend to ignore all but the most obvious signs of life in an abortion baby.

In the November 1974 newsletter of the International Correspondence Society of Obstetricians and Gynecologists, several doctors addressed a question from a practitioner who had written in an earlier issue that he was troubled by what to do when an aborted infant showed signs of life.

One was Dr. Ronald Bolognese, an obstetrician at Pennsylvania Hospital in Philadelphia, who replied:

"At the time of delivery, it has been our policy to wrap the fetus in a towel. The fetus is then moved to another room while our attention is turned to the care of [the woman]. She is examined to determine whether complete placental expulsion has occurred and the extent of vaginal bleeding. Once we are sure that her condition is stable, the fetus is evaluated. Almost invariably all signs of life have ceased."

(Bolognese recanted that statement in a 1979 interview, "That's not what we do now," he said. "We would transport it to the intensive care nursery.")

In addition, Dr. William Brenner of the University of North Carolina Medical School suggested that if breathing and movement persist for several minutes, "the patient's physician, if he is not in attendance, should probably be contacted and informed of the situation. The pediatrician on call should probably be apprised of the situation if signs of life continue."

Dr. Warren Pearse, executive director of the American College of Obstetrics and Gynecology, was asked in a 1979 interview what doctors do, as standard practice, to check whether an aborted fetus is alive.

"What you would do next [after expulsion] is nothing," Pearse said. "You assume the infant is dead unless it shows signs of life. You're dealing with a dead fetus unless there is sustained cardiac action or sustained respiration—it's not enough if there's a single heartbeat or an occasional gasp."

These seemingly callous policies are based on the assumption that abortion babies are too small or too damaged by the abortion process to survive and live meaningful lives. That is not necessarily the case, though, even for babies set aside and neglected in the minutes after delivery.

A nursing supervisor who asked not to be identified told of an abortion live birth in the mid-'70s in a Florida hospital. The infant was dumped in a bedpan without examination, as was standard practice. "It did not die," the nurse said. "It was left in the bedpan for an hour before signs of life were noticed. It weighed slightly over a pound."

The baby remained in critical condition for several months, but excellent care in a unit for premature infants enabled it to survive. The child, now 5 years old, was put up for adoption. The nursing supervisor, who has followed its progress, said she has pictures of the youngster "riding a bicycle and playing a little piano."

In the spring of 1979 two babies were born alive, five weeks apart, after saline abortions at the Wilmington Medical Center. They were given vigorous care, survived and were later adopted. One had been discovered by a nurse, struggling for breath and with a faint heartbeat, after having been placed in a plastic specimen jar. The second was judged to be a live delivery and was given immediate help breathing.

A baby girl, weighing 1 pound 11 ounces, was born in February 1979 after a saline abortion at Inglewood (Calif.) Hospital. Harbor General Hospital, which is associated with UCLA and is fully equipped to care for premature babies, was called for help, but the neonatal rescue team did not respond. The infant died after three hours.

The Los Angeles Department of Health Services investigated and was told that there had been confusion over the baby's weight and that it reportedly showed poor vital signs. It was "very unusual for them not to pick up [an infant] of this size," Dr. Rosemary Leake of Harbor General told investigators.

The administrator of a New York abortion unit, asked what would be done for a live-born abortion baby, said, "The nurses have been trained in how to handle this. I'd like to think we would do everything to save it. But honestly I'm not sure."

These incidents together suggest that life in an aborted infant may or may not be recognized. If it is, supportive treatment may or may not be ordered.

Such incidents, when discovered, often provoke prosecutions. A few may seem something like murder at first blush. But on closer inspection the doctors' actions have been judged, time and again, not quite to fit the definition of a crime.

Nowhere was this more vividly shown than in the case of Dr. Jesse J. Floyd, who was indicted on charges of murder and criminal abortion by a grand jury in Columbia, S.C., in August 1975. The charges were the result of an abortion a year earlier of a baby that appeared to have a gestational age of 27 to 28 weeks. It weighed 2 pounds 5 ounces and lived for 20 days.

In October 1979 the state dropped its case against Floyd. County prosecutor James C. Anders later conceded in an interview that South Carolina's abortion law was of dubious constitutionality. "In the second place," he said, "I had a reluctant witness [the infant's mother]. That and the passage of time worked against me."

A detailed record was developed in the case, as part of a federal suit that Floyd brought against Anders in which he sought to block the state prosecution. The 20-year-old mother, Louise A., lived in the small town of Hopkins, worked at a military-base commissary and had plans to enroll in a technical college. Those plans made her unwilling to have the baby she was carrying, so she presented herself for an abortion at Floyd's office in July 1974. Court records indicate that she had been told erroneously by her hometown doctor's nurse that she was not pregnant, and that she only slowly realized that she was.

Floyd found her to be past the first trimester of pregnancy, and under South Carolina law that meant an in-hospital abortion would be required. There were delays in her raising $450 for the abortion and more delays in admitting her to Richland Memorial Hospital. She was injected with prostaglandin on Sept. 4 and expelled the live baby early on the morning of Sept. 6.

"I started having real bad labor pains again," Louise recalled in her deposition, "and finally my baby was born. I called the nurse. Then about four or five of them came in the room at the time. The head nurse came in the same time the other nurses came in and she told me did I know that the baby was a seven-month baby. I told her no.

"One of the nurses said that the baby was alive. They took the baby out of the room. He never did cry, he just made some kind of a noise."

The first doctor on the scene, paged from the cafeteria, was a young resident. She did not hesitate. On detecting a heartbeat of 100, she clamped and severed the umbilical cord and had the baby sent to the hospital's intensive care unit.

"It was a shock, a totally unique emergency situation, very upsetting to all of us," the doctor, who now practices in California, said in an interview. "Some people have disagreed with me [about ordering intensive care for an abortion live birth] but that seems to me the only way you can go.

"It's like watching a drowning. You act. You don't have the luxury of calling around and consulting. You institute life-preserving measures first and decide about viability later on."

Ten days after birth, the baby had improved markedly and was given a 50-50 chance of survival. Then he developed a tear in the small intestine and died of that and other complications on Sept. 26.

Louise A. never saw the child. She checked out of the hospital two days after the abortion and did not return. But she did show a passing interest in the baby's progress.

"I kept calling this nurse," Louise said in her deposition. "I would call . . . and get information from them about the baby, and they told me he was doing fine. They told me he had picked up two or three pounds. I started going to school, and one afternoon I called home and they told me the baby had died, but no one told me the cause of his death."

Floyd never saw the infant either. On the day of the abortion, his hospital privileges at Richland were withdrawn, and they have never been restored.

These circumstances presented prosecutor Anders with a difficult case. Floyd had had no physical contact with the live-born infant, nor was he issuing orders concerning its care. Nonetheless, Anders thought the doctor could be held responsible for the infant's death.

Anders pressed his murder charge using an old English common-law theory. Under this theory, willfully doing damage to a "vital" infant in the womb could be considered a crime against the fetus as a person. The abortion itself, Anders alleged, was an assault.

The line of argument is not entirely farfetched. For instance, a Camden, N.J., man was convicted of murder in 1975 after he shot a woman in the abdomen late in her pregnancy, causing the death of the twins she was carrying. But application of the theory to abortion had never been tested—in South Carolina or anywhere else.

South Carolina law in the mid-1970s prohibited third-trimester abortion unless two other doctors certified that the abortion was essential to protect the life or health of the mother. No such certifications were made for Louise. However, various Supreme Court rulings suggested that both the requirement of consultation with other doctors and the explicit definition of viability (as beginning in the third trimester) would make that law unconstitutional.

Floyd's lawyers, George Kosko of Columbia, S.C., and Roy Lucas of Washington, also filed voluminous expert affidavits on the difficulty of estimating gestational age accurately. At worst, they argued, Floyd had made a mistaken diagnosis. What proof was there that he had intentionally aborted a viable baby?

District Court Judge Robert Chapman and the Fourth Circuit Court of Appeals agreed that the prosecution was based on flimsy evidence and should be blocked. However, the Supreme Court disagreed, in a ruling in March 1979, and suggested that judgment should be withheld on constitutional matters until the state prosecution had run its course. The way was thus cleared for Anders to proceed, but with witnesses dispersed, memories fading and the legal basis for prosecution still doubtful, Anders chose to drop the case.

Floyd, 49, continues performing first-trimester abortions at his Ladies Clinic, but the loss of hospital privileges and the damage to his reputation caused his surgical practice to collapse, he said.

The long legal proceeding also seems to have had a chilling effect on abortion practice throughout South Carolina, which Anders concedes was one of his intentions.

"The main thing is the dilemma it puts the other physicians in," Floyd said in an interview. "It's just about dried up second-trimester abortions in this state. I have to send mine to Atlanta, Washington or New York."

Asked about late abortions and the risk of live births, Floyd said he thought abortions performed through the sixth month of pregnancy create "a problem to which there isn't an answer. We probably need to move back to 20 weeks. I would be reluctant to do one now after 20 weeks."

A similar case occurred about the same time in South Carolina, when Anders obtained a criminal indictment charging Dr. Herbert Schreiber of Camden, S.C., with first-degree murder and illegal abortion.

On July 18, 1976, a month after the charges had been filed, the 60-year-old doctor was found dead in a motel room in Asheville, N.C. A motel maid discovered the body slumped in a chair. Several bottles of prescription drugs were recovered from the room. Two days later the Buncombe County medical examiner ruled the death a suicide from a drug overdose.

Schreiber, who left no note, had pleaded not guilty to the charge of having killed a live baby girl after an abortion by choking or smothering her to death.

Comparing the Floyd and Schreiber cases, Anders found an irony: Schreiber "just reached in and strangled the baby," the prosecutor said his evidence showed. "I charged him with murder, and he committed suicide. If he had been willing to wait, he probably would have been OK too."

Not every doctor who performs a late abortion has to confront an aggressive prosecutor like Anders. But even those abortion live births that escape public notice raise deeply troubling emotions for the medical personnel involved. "Our training disciplines you to follow the doctor's orders," explained a California maternity nurse. "If you do something on your own for the baby that the doctor has not ordered and that may not meet with his commitment to his patient, the mother can sue you. A nurse runs a grave risk if she acts on her own. Not only her immediate job but her license may be threatened."

Nonetheless, nursing staffs have led a number of quiet revolts against late abortions. Two major hospitals in the Fort Lauderdale areas, for instance, stopped offering abortions in the late 1970s after protests from nurses who felt uncomfortable handling the lifelike fetuses.

A Grand Rapids, Mich., hospital stopped late-term abortions in 1977 after nurses made good on their threat not to handle the fetuses. One night they left a stillborn fetus lying in its mother's bed for an hour and a half, despite angry calls from the attending physician, who finally went in and removed it himself.

In addition, a number of hospital administrators have reported problems in mixing maternity and abortion patients—the latter must listen to the cries of newborn infants while waiting for the abortion to work. And it has proved difficult in general hospitals to provide round-the-clock staffing of obstetrical nurses willing to assist with the procedure.

One young nurse in the Midwest, who quit to go into teaching, remembers "a happy group of nurses" turning nasty to each other and the physicians because of conflicts over abortion. One day, she recalled, a woman physician "walked out of the operating room after doing six abortions. She smeared her hand [which was covered with blood] on mine and said, 'Go wash it off. That's the hand that did it.' "

Several studies have documented the distress that late abortion causes many nurses. Dr. Warren M. Hern, chief physician, and Billie Corrigan, head nurse, of the Boulder (Colo.) Abortion Clinic, presented a paper to a 1978 Planned Parenthood convention entitled "What About Us? Staff Reactions . . ."

The clinic, one of the largest in the Rocky Mountain states, specializes in the D&E (dilation and evacuation) method of second-trimester abortion, a procedure in which the fetus is cut from the womb in pieces. Hern and Corrigan reported that eight of the 15 staff members surveyed reported emotional problems. Two said they worried about the physician's psychological well-being. Two reported horrifying dreams about fetuses, one of which involved the hiding of fetal parts so that other people would not see them.

"We have produced an unusual dilemma," Hern and Corrigan concluded. "A procedure is rapidly becoming recognized as the procedure of choice in late abortion, but those capable of performing or assisting with the procedure are having strong personal reservations about participating in an operation which they view as destructive and violent."

Dr. Julius Butler, a professor of obstetrics and gynecology at the University of Minnesota Medical School, is concerned about studies suggesting that D&E is the safest method and should be used more widely. "Remember," he said, "there is a human being at the other end of the table taking that kid apart.

"We've had guys drinking too much, taking drugs, even a suicide or two. There have been no studies I know of of the problem, but the unwritten kind of statistics we see are alarming."

"You are doing a destructive process," said Dr. William Benbow Thompson of the University of California at Irvine. "Arms, legs, chests come out in the forceps. It's not a sight for everybody."

Not all doctors think the stressfulness is overwhelming. The procedure "is a little bit unpleasant for the physician," concludes Dr. Mildred Hanson, a petite woman in her early 50s who does eight to 10 abortions a day in a clinic in Minneapolis, just a few miles across town from where Butler works. "It's easier to . . . leave someone else—namely a nurse—to be with the patient and do the dirty work.

"There is a lot in medicine that is unpleasant" but necessary—like amputating a leg—she argues, and doctors shouldn't let their own squeamishness deprive patients of a procedure that's cheaper and less traumatic.

However, Dr. Nancy Kaltreider, an academic psychiatrist at the University of San Francisco, has found in several studies "an unexpectedly strong reaction" by the assisting staff to late-abortion procedures. For nurses, she hypothesizes, handling tissues that resemble a fully formed baby "runs directly against the medical emphasis on preserving life."

The psychological wear-and-tear from doing late abortions is obvious. Philadelphia's Dr. Bolognese, who seven years ago was recommending wrapping abortion live-borns in a towel, has stopped doing late abortions.

"You get burned out," he said. Noting that his main research interest is in the management of complicated obstetrical cases, he observed: "It seemed kind of schizophrenic, to be doing that on the one hand [helping women with problem pregnancies to have babies] and do abortions."

Dr. John Franklin, medical director of Planned Parenthood of Southeastern Pennsylvania, was the plaintiff in a 1979 Supreme Court case liberalizing the limits on late abortions. He does not do such procedures himself. "I find them pretty heavy weather both for myself and for my patients," he said in an interview.

Dr. Kerenyi, the New York abortion expert, who is at Mt. Sinai Hospital, has similar feelings but reaches a different conclusion. "I first of all take pride in my deliveries. But I've seen a lot of bad outcomes in women who did not want their babies—so I think we should help women who want to get rid of them. I find I can live with this dual role."

The legal jeopardy, the emotional strain, the winking neglect with which "signs of life" must be met—all these things nurture secrecy. Late abortions take place "behind a white curtain," as one prosecutor put it, well sheltered from public view.

Only one large-scale study has been done of live births after abortions—by George Stroh and Dr. Alan Hinman in upstate New York from July 1970 through December 1972 (a period during which abortion was legal in New York alone). It turned up 38 cases of live births in a sample of 150,000 abortions.

Other studies, including one that found signs of life in about 10 percent of the prostaglandin abortions at a Hartford, Conn., hospital, date from the mid-1970s. No one is so naive as to think there is reliable voluntary reporting of live births in the present climate, according to Dr. Cates of the Center for Disease Control.

Evidence gathered during research for this story suggests, without proving definitively, that much of the traffic in later abortions now flows to the New York and Los Angeles metropolitan areas, where loose practice more easily escapes notice.

"The word has spread," the *Daily Breeze,* a small Los Angeles suburban paper, said in July 1980, "that facilities in greater Los Angeles will do late abortions. How late only the woman and the doctor who performs them know."

This kind of thing is disturbing even to some people with a strong orientation in favor of legal abortion. For instance, the Philadelphia office of CHOICE, which describes itself as "a reproductive health advocacy agency," will recommend only Dr. Kerenyi's service at Mt. Sinai among the half-dozen in New York offering abortion up to 24 weeks. The others have shortcomings in safety, sanitation or professional standards, in the agency's view.

An internal investigation of the abortion unit at Jewish Memorial Hospital in Manhattan, showed that six fetuses aborted there in the summer of 1979 weighed more than 1⅓ pounds. The babies were not alive, but were large enough to be potentially viable. A state health inspector found in June 1979 that the unit had successfully aborted a fetus that was well over a foot long and appeared to be of 32 weeks gestation. Hospital officials confirmed in an interview that later in 1979 a fetus weighing more than four pounds had been aborted.

"It's disconcerting," Iona Siegel, administrator of the Women's Health Center at Kingsbrook Jewish Medical Center in Brooklyn, said of abortions performed so late that the infant is viable. When Ms. Siegel hears, as she says she often does, that a patient turned away by Kingsbrook because she was past 24 weeks of pregnancy had an abortion somewhere else, "that makes me angry. Number one, it's against the law. Number two, it's dangerous to the health of the mother."

Though one might expect organized medicine to take a hand in bringing some order to the practice of late abortions, that is not happening.

"We're not really very pro-abortion," said Dr. Ervin Nichols, director of practice activities for the American College of Obstetrics and Gynecology. "As a matter of fact, anything beyond 20 weeks, we're kind of upset about it."

If abortions after 20 weeks are a dubious practice, how does that square with abortion up to 24 weeks being offered openly in Los Angeles and New York and advertised in newspapers and the Yellow Pages there and elsewhere?

"That's not medicine," Nichols replied. "That's hucksterism."

Cates, of the Center for Disease Control, concedes that he has ambivalent feelings about those who do the very late procedures. There is obviously some profiteering and some bending of state laws forbidding abortions in the third trimester. But since late abortions are hard to get legally in many places, Cates puts a low priority on trying to police such practices. Medical authorities leave the late-abortion practitioners to do what they will. And so, too, by necessity, do the legal authorities.

The Supreme Court framed its January 1973 opinion legalizing abortion around the slippery concept of viability. As defined by Justice Harry Blackmun in the landmark *Roe* v. *Wade* case, viability occurs when the fetus is "potentially able to live outside the mother's womb albeit with artificial aid."

The court granted women an unrestricted right to abortions, as an extension to their right of privacy, in the first trimester of pregnancy. From that point to viability, the state can regulate abortions only to make sure they are safe. And only after a fetus reaches viability can state law limit abortion and protect the "rights" of the fetus.

"Viability," Blackmun wrote, after a summer spent researching the matter in the library of the Mayo Clinic, "is usually placed at about seven months (28 weeks) but may occur earlier, even at 24 weeks."

The standard was meant to be elastic, changing in time with medical advances. Blackmun took no particular account, though, of the possibility of abortion live births, or of errors in estimating gestational age.

In subsequent cases, the high court ruled that:

A Missouri law was too specific in forbidding abortion after 24 weeks. "It is not the proper function of the legislature or the court," Blackmun wrote, "to place viability, which essentially is a medical concept, at a specific point in the gestational period."

A Pennsylvania law was too vague. The law banned abortions "if there is sufficient reason to believe that the fetus may be viable." The court said it was wrong to put doctors in jeopardy without giving them clearer notice of what they must do.

State laws could not interfere with a doctor's professional judgment by dictating the choice of procedure for late abortions or by requiring aggressive care of abortion live births.

According to a 1979 survey by Jeanie Rosoff of Planned Parenthood's Alan Guttmacher Institute, 30 states have laws regulating third-trimester abortions. Some of these laws prohibit or strictly limit abortions after the fetus has reached viability. Some require doctors to try to save abortion live-born babies. Only a few states have both types of laws.

In addition, a number of these laws have been found unconstitutional. Others obviously would be, in light of Supreme Court rulings. Virtually all the state laws would be subject to constitutional challenge if used as the basis of prosecution against an individual doctor.

New York and California, ironically, have among the strongest, most detailed laws mandating care for survivors of abortions. But these laws have proved only a negligible check on the abortion of viable babies.

"We've had a number of claims come up that a baby was born live and full effort was not given to saving it," said Dr. Michael Baden, former chief medical examiner of New York City. "We've not had cases of alleged strangulation (as with Dr. Waddill in California) and that surely must be rare. All [the doctor] has to do is nothing and the result is the same."

Alan Marrus, a Bronx County assistant district attorney, has investigated several live-birth cases and the applicable New York law. He has yet to find "a case that presented us with facts that warranted prosecution. You need an expert opinion that in fact there was life and that the fetus would have survived. Often the fetus has been destroyed—so there is nothing for your expert witness to examine."

The incidents only come to light at all, Baden and Marrus noted, if some whistle-blower inside the hospital or clinic brings them to the attention of the legal authorities. The credibility of that sort of witness may be subject to attack. And even if the facts do weigh against a doctor, he has some resources left. Almost always he can claim to have made no more than a good-faith error in medical judgment.

"This is happening all over the place" said a California prosecutor. "Babies that should live are dying because callous physicians let them die." But he despairs of winning any convictions. "Nobody's as dumb as Waddill. They're smarter today. They know how to cover themselves."

Unfortunately, advances in medical technique may only aggravate the overall problem. Fetuses are becoming viable earlier and earlier, while the demand for later abortions shows no signs of abating. Some argue that Justice Blackmun's definition of viability as "usually seven months" was obsolete the day it was published. It clearly is now.

A decade ago, survival of an infant less than 3 pounds or 30 weeks gestation was indeed rare, principally because the lungs of smaller infants, unaided, are too undeveloped and fragile to sustain life. Now infants with birth weights of about 1⅔ pounds routinely survive with the best of care, according to Dr. Richard Behrman, chief of neonatology at Rainbow Babies and Children's Hospital in Cleveland and chairman of a national commission that studied viability in the mid-1970s.

Sometimes even smaller babies make it, and the idea that most of them will be retarded or disabled is out-of-date, Behrman said. "Most . . . survive intact."

Even with the medical advances, though, some live-born infants are simply too small and undeveloped to have a realistic chance to survive. A survey last year of specialists in neonatal care found that 90 percent would not order life-support by machine for babies smaller than 1 pound 2 ounces or less than 24 weeks gestation. And on occasion, a newborn may manifest muscular twitches or gasping movements without ever "being alive" according to the usual legal test of drawing a breath that fills the lungs.

Still, it is no longer a miracle for an infant of 24 weeks development (which can be legally aborted) to be saved if born prematurely.

"It is frightening," said Dr. Roger K. Freeman, medical director of Women's Hospital at the Long Beach Memorial Medical Center in Long Beach, Calif. "Medical advances in the treatment of premature babies enable us to save younger fetuses than ever before. When a fetus survives an abortion, however, there may be a collision of tragic proportions between medicine and maternity. Medicine is now able to give the premature a chance that may be rejected by the mother."

In 1970, Freeman developed the fetal stress test, a widely used technique for monitoring the heart rate of unborn fetuses. Also, he and a colleague at Long Beach, Dr. Houchang D. Mondalou, have developed a drug, betamethzene, that matures premature lungs within days instead of weeks. The hospital claims a 90 percent success rate with infants weighing as little as 1 pound 11 ounces.

At the University of California at Irvine, work is under way on an "artificial placenta" that doctors there say could, within five years, push the threshold of viability back even further.

The life-saving techniques are not exclusive to top academic hospitals, either. Good neonatal care is now broadly available across the United States. In fact, the lively issue in medical circles these days is not whether tiny premature babies can be saved, but whether it is affordable. Bills for the full course of treatment of a two-pound infant typically run between $25,000 and $100,000. To some, that seems a lot to pay, especially in the case of an abortion baby that was not wanted in the first place.

The only way out of the dilemma, it would seem,

would be for fewer women to seek late abortions. Though some optimists argue that this is happening, there is evidence that it is not.

Studies show that women seeking abortions late in the second trimester are often young, poor and sexually ignorant. Many either fail to realize they are pregnant or delay telling their families out of fear at the reaction. The patients also include those who have had a change of circumstance or a change of heart after deciding initially to carry through a pregnancy; some of these women are disturbed.

As first-trimester abortion and sex education become more widely available, the optimists' argument goes, nearly all women who choose abortion will get an early abortion. But in fact a new class of older, well-educated, affluent women has now joined the hardship cases in seeking late abortions.

This is because a recently developed technique, amniocentesis, allows genetic screening of the unborn fetus for various hereditary diseases. Through this screening, a woman can learn whether the child she is carrying is free of such dreaded conditions as Downs syndrome (mongolism) or Tay-Sachs disease, a genetic disorder that is always fatal, early in childhood.

The test involves drawing off a sample of amniotic fluid, in which the fetus is immersed in the womb. This cannot be done until the 15th or 16th week. Test cultures for the various potential problems take several weeks to grow. Sometimes the result is inconclusive and the test must be repeated. The testing also reveals the unborn child's sex and can be used to detect minor genetic imperfections.

To many women, particularly those over 35, anmiocentesis seems a rational approach to minimizing the chances of bearing a defective child. A few, according to published reports, go a step further and make sure the baby is the sex they want before deciding to bear the child.

In any case, it is late in the second trimester—within weeks of the current threshold of viability—before the information becomes available on which a decision is made to abort or not abort. The squeeze will intensify as amniocentesis becomes more widely available and as smaller and smaller infants are able to survive.

The abortion live-birth dilemma has caught the attention of several experts on medical ethics, and they have proposed two possible solutions.

The simplest, advocated by Dr. Sissela Bok of the Harvard Medical School among others, is just to prohibit late abortions. Taking into account the possible errors in estimating gestational age, she argues, the cutoff should be set well before the earliest gestational age at which infants are surviving.

Using exactly this reasoning, several European countries—France and Sweden, for example—have made abortions readily available in the first three months of pregnancy but very difficult to get thereafter. The British, at the urging of Sir John Peel, an influential physician-statesman, have considered in each of the last three years moving the cutoff date from 28 weeks to 20 weeks, but so far have not done so.

But in this country, the Supreme Court has applied a different logic in defining the abortion right, and the groups that won that right would not cheerfully accept a retreat now.

A second approach, advocated by Mrs. Bok and others, is to define the woman's abortion right as being only a right to terminate the pregnancy, not to have the fetus dead. Then if the fetus is born live, it is viewed as a person in its own right, entitled to care appropriate to its condition.

This "progressive" principle is encoded in the policies of many hospitals and the laws of some states, including New York and California. As the record shows, though, in the alarming event of an actual live birth, doctors on the scene may either observe the principle or ignore it.

And the concept even strikes some who do abortions as misguided idealism.

"You have to have a feticidal dose" of saline solution, said Dr. Kerenyi of Mt. Sinai in New York. "It's almost a breach of contract not to. Otherwise, what are you going to do—hand her back a baby having done it questionable damage? I say, if you can't do it, don't do it."

The scenario Kerenyi describes did in fact happen, in March 1978 in Cleveland. A young woman entered Mt. Sinai Hospital there for an abortion. The baby was born live and, after several weeks of intensive care at Rainbow Babies and Children's Hospital, the child went home—with its mother.

The circumstances were so extraordinary that medical personnel broke the code of confidentiality and discussed the case with friends. Spokeswomen for the two hospitals confirmed the sequence of events. Mother and child returned to Rainbow for checkup when the child was 14 months old, the spokeswoman there said, and both were doing fine.

The mother could not be reached for comment. But a source familiar with the case remembered one detail: "The doctors had a very hard time making her realize she had a child. She kept saying, 'But I had an abortion.' "

Of the various ways to perform an abortion after the midpoint of pregnancy, there is only one that never, ever results in live births.

It is D&E (dilation and evacuation), and not only is it foolproof, but many researchers consider it safer, cheaper and less unpleasant for the patient. However, it is particularly stressful to medical personnel. That is because D&E requires literally cutting the fetus from the womb and, then, reassembling the parts, or at least keeping them all in view, to assure that the abortion is complete.

Ten years ago it was considered reckless to do an abortion with cutting instruments after the first trimester of pregnancy. Now, improved instruments, more skilled practitioners and laminaria—bands of seaweed that expand when moist and are used to gently dilate the cervix, creating an opening through which to extract fetal parts—allow the technique to be used much later.

D&E is being hailed as extending the safe and easy techniques used for first-trimester abortions (cutting or vacuuming out the contents of the womb) well into the second three months of pregnancy. But there are dissenters. Dr. Bernard Nathanson, formerly a top New York City abortionist, now an anti-abortion author and lecturer, says that D&E "is a very dangerous technique in the hands of anyone less than highly skilled."

Besides, D&E puts all the emotional burden on the physicians. And there are other techniques that allow the doctor, as one physician put it, to "stick a needle in the [patient's] tummy," then leave the patient to deliver the fetus vaginally as in normal childbirth and nurses to assist and clean up.

These more common methods for abortion after the midpoint of pregnancy use the instillation of either saline solution or prostaglandin. In these procedures, some of the woman's nurturing amniotic fluid is drawn out of the womb by an injection through her belly and is replaced with the abortion-inducing drug. (The amount of fluid in the womb is kept relatively constant to make sure the womb does not rupture.)

The two instillation substances work in different ways. Saline solution poisons the fetus, probably through ingestion, though the process is not completely understood. Usually within six hours, the fetal heartbeat stops. At the same time, the saline induces labor, though supplemental doses of other labor-inducing drugs often are given to speed this effect.

Prostaglandin, on the other hand, is a distillate of the chemical substance that causes muscles to move. It is thought not to affect the fetus directly but instead is potent at inducing labor. Fetal death, if it does occur, is from prematurity and the trauma of passage through the birth canal.

Each substance also has an undesired side effect. Saline, an anti-coagulant that increases bleeding, can make minor bleeding problems more serious and in rare cases even cause death. Prostaglandin, because it causes muscles to contract indiscriminately, was found to cause vomiting and diarrhea in more than half the patients in early tests. Claims that it causes fewer major complications, which made it preferred to saline by many in the mid-1970s, have now been questioned. And the high incidence of live births (40 times more frequent than with saline, according to one study) also has lessened its popularity.

But saline is not foolproof either in preventing live births. Dr. Thomas F. Kerenyi of Mt. Sinai Hospital in New York, the best-known researcher on saline abortions, said most live births result from "errors in techniques"— either administering too small a dosage or getting some of it into the wrong part of the womb.

A wrong estimation of gestational age can cause either a saline or prostaglandin abortion to fail. A larger-than-expected fetus might survive the trauma of labor or might reject a dose of saline (or urea, a third instillation substance sometimes used).

And on the basis of physical examination alone, studies show, doctors miss the correct gestational age by two weeks in one case out of five, by four weeks in one case out of 100, and sometimes by more than that. Pregnancies can be dated more exactly by a sonogram, a test that produces an outline image of the fetus in the womb, but because of its cost (about $100) many doctors continue to rely on physical exams.

There is one other abortion technique, hysterotomy, but it is the least desirable of all from several points of view. Because it is invasive surgery (identical to a Caesarean section), it has a much higher rate of complication than do the installation techniques. Usually done only after attempts to abort with saline have failed, it has the highest incidence of all of live births.

As the infant is lifted from the womb, said one obstetrician, "he is only sleeping, like his mother. She is under anesthesia, and so is he. You want to know how they kill him? They put a towel over his face so he can't breathe. And by the time they get him to the lab, he is dead."

Over the years, the chief criterion in choosing between abortion methods have been safety for the patient. Advocates of D&E contend that bleeding, perforation of the uterus and infection all occur less frequently with D&E than with other methods. Dr. Willard Cates of the Center for Disease Control in Atlanta prefers D&E. Because it can be done—unlike instillation—in the early part of the second trimester, he has said, the need for as many as 80 percent of the very late abortions could be eliminated.

How very late are abortions performed?

His own clinic at Mt. Sinai, Dr. Kerenyi said, screens patients closely to make sure they are not past the legal 24-week limit. But in theory, he said, there is nothing to prevent successful saline abortions from being performed "virtually all the way to birth. At 30 weeks, say, you would just have to draw off and inject that much more of the solution."

Most practitioners who were interviewed say they stop doing D&E at 18 to 22 weeks. But again, there appears to be nothing to prevent the technique from being used much later.

"You can do it, you can do it," an abortionist, who would talk only if not quoted by name, said of D&Es late in pregnancy. "Some son-of-a-bitch misreads a sonogram and sends me a woman 26 weeks. I've done it. You've just got to take your time and be careful. And you're not going to end up with a live birth."

Nurses are the ones who bear the burden of handling the human-looking products of late abortions. And when an unintentional live birth occurs, they are the first to confront the waving of limbs and the gasping.

Reluctant to talk about their experiences, most of those interviewed for this article did not want their names to be published, and out of professional loyalty, they did not even want their hospitals to be named.

They spoke of being deeply troubled by what they have seen of late abortions in American hospitals.

Linda is a nurse in her late 50s in Southern California. Hurrying out of a patient's room one day to dispose of the aborted "tissue," as nurses were taught to think of it, she felt movement. Startled, she looked down, straight into the staring eyes of a live baby.

"It looked right at me," she recalled. "This baby had real big eyes. It looked at you like it was saying, 'Do something—do something.' Those haunting eyes. Oh God, I still remember them."

She rushed the 1½-pound infant to the nursing station. She took the heart rate—80 to 100 beats a minute. She timed the respirations—three to four breaths a minute. She called the doctor.

"I called him because the baby was breathing," Linda said. "It was pink. It had a heartbeat. The doctor told me the baby was not viable and to send it to the lab. I said, 'But it's breathing' and he said, 'It's non-viable, it won't be breathing long—send it to the lab.' "

She did not follow the order. Nor did she have resources at her command to provide any life-saving care. Two hours later the infant died, still at the nursing station, still without medical treatment. It died in a makeshift crib with one hot-water bottle for warmth and an open tube of oxygen blowing near its head.

The nursing supervisor, Linda said, had refused to let her put the baby in the nursery, where there was equipment to assist premature babies in distress. "She said to follow the doctor's orders and take it to the lab. I kept it with me at the station. We couldn't do an awful lot for it."

This happened eight years ago, in 1973, but Linda is still upset. "I stood by and watched that baby die without doing a thing," she said. "I have guilt feelings to this day. I feel the baby might have lived had it been properly cared for."

Jane, about 50, is the head floor nurse in an Ohio hospital. She and her fellow nurses successfully petitioned their hospital in 1978 to stop doing late abortions. Twice before that, she witnessed live births after abortions.

She recalls vividly the 16-year-old patient who phoned her mother after her abortion and said in an agonized voice, "Ma, it's out—but Ma, it's alive."

That happened in 1975. Jane still speaks of it bitterly, her eyes flashing anger.

A year earlier Jane saw the second abortion live birth in her experience. "I was called by the patient's roommate," she recalled. "When I got there the baby's head was sticking out and its little tongue was wiggling. Everybody felt they couldn't do anything until they called the doctor. It was a little thing—it only lasted about 15 minutes. But it was alive, and we did nothing. And that was wrong."

It rankles, too, that she was routinely forced to handle dead fetuses, the size and shape of well-formed premature babies.

"Because of my position," she said, "I had to pick them up off the bed and put them in a bottle of formalin [a preservative fluid]. Sometimes you had to have a very large container. Our gynecologists seemed to have a very poor ability to estimate gestational age. Time and again they would say with a straight face, 'This woman is 20 weeks pregnant' when she was actually 26 weeks."

Norma Rojo, about 35, is an obstetrical nurse at Indio Community Hospital in Indio, Calif. She was present the night of May 3, 1980, when a 15-year-old patient delivered a live baby girl after a saline abortion.

"Get rid of it" the patient cried hysterically. "I'm sorry. Mama—get rid of it," she said, the baby alive, kicking and crying between her legs.

Two weeks earlier the girl had been in a traffic accident that killed four others and had sought the abortion out of fear that her baby might be damaged.

The fetus, which in tests had shown a normal heartbeat of 132 to 136 in the womb, appeared healthy at birth. "She was beautiful," said Mrs. Rojo. "She was pink. There were no physical deformities. She let out a little lusty cry. She lay in a basin put there to catch all the stuff. She was waving her arms and legs. You could tell she was making a big effort to live."

The nurses cut the umbilical cord, wrapped the infant in a blanket and took her to the intensive care nursery. She was put in an isolette (a life-support system) within minutes and was given oxygen.

Acting on their own, the nurses had the 1 pound 14 ounce baby transferred six hours later to Loma Linda University Medical Center, one of several hospitals in the Los Angeles area specializing in the care of very small premature infants. Four days later the baby was reported stable but had developed a complication causing hemorrhaging of the brain. Dr. David Deming of Loma Linda said then that its chances were only 50-50. He added, though, that the abortion had done little damage. "I would say there is probably no effect on her from the saline."

Eleven days after birth, the baby died. Family members indicated they were upset by the nurses' effort to save it.

"After this experience," Rojo said, "my friend [another nurse] and I are changed. We realize doctors aren't perfect. . . . I hope that this is the last [abortion live birth] I ever see, but if there are any more, we will do the same thing."

Notes

Chapter 1

[1]If you doubt you've been affected by this conditioning, answer this question: Are you surprised to learn that Phyllis Schlafly, the anti-ERA spokesman, did graduate work at Harvard University?

[2]This decline has often been Christians' own fault. Elsewhere in *Addicted to Mediocrity* (Westchester, Ill.: Crossway Books, 1981) I dealt with the reasons for this decline in influence.

[3]See the author's *Plan For Action* (Old Tappan, NJ: Revell, 1981).

[4]Time, Inc. may not yet be able to reconcile itself to the sexual abuse of children but it seems that the New York Superior Court can, in a recent ruling that found child pornography legal on "constitutional" grounds!

[5]Read John W. Whitehead's *The Second American Revolution* (Elgin, Ill.: David C. Cook, 1982) for the definitive argument of this point.

[6]Jerry Falwell was offered the "My Turn" page only after a storm of protest to *Newsweek* over their incredibly biased and consistently bigoted reporting on him. Mr. Cal Thomas, vice-president of the Moral Majority, wrote to the publisher decrying this style of one-sided journalism, and finally the amount of protest resulted in a chance to answer. It pays to speak up.

[7]As an example of this, consider the ACLU. Bringing more than six thousand suits a year, the ACLU virtually dominates the legal system in terms of social change through court action. Many of its cases are against the "establishment of religion"; in other words, against Judeo-Christian influence within society. The ACLU functions with impunity, gradually curbing religious freedom, while imposing by force of law secular humanism and left-wing ideology on the population. All this in the name of constitutionalism and freedom, no less! Not to mention the fact that many judges hearing the cases as former ACLU members virtually are little more than rubber stamps in their "decisions."

[8]Harvey Cox, *The Secular City* (New York: Macmillan, 1965).

[9]As John Whitehead notes in *The Second American Revolution* (D. C. Cook, 1982):

> Any legal system, secular or otherwise, must develop a religious foundation of law, and maintain that foundation by hostility to any other law order. Therefore, "there can be no tolerance in a law system for another religion." In the latter part of

the nineteenth century and early twentieth century the American legal order released its hostility against the theistic foundation of American law and developed a secular humanist religion to replace it. Because tolerance is non-existent, the obvious consequence is either open or subtle hostility or persecution of the former theistic foundation of law. The Supreme Court's theory of neutrality by the State is merely a hopeful illusion.

Chapter 2

[1]Material quoted is adapted from *Public Opinion* and reprinted in the *Indianapolis Star*, January 25, 1982, p. 7.

[2]Tom Johnson, the publisher of the *Los Angeles Times*, reflecting on the responsibility of the press in the fourth annual Frank E. Gannet Lecture, reminded his audience: "In the more than 1,500 cities in this country with daily newspapers, fewer than 50 have two or more under competing ownership. The 10 largest newspaper chains, including the one I represent, have one-third of the nation's total readership. . . . And the influence of the major networks may be even more pervasive."

[3]When one can have the word "religious" coupled with "abortion rights," then truly language has lost its meaning.

[4]"Propaganda," as we have come to define it in our time, includes the connotation of deliberately distorting facts and appealing to the prejudices and baser motivations of an audience in order to win their support and approval for an undeserving institution or cause. It's an extended form of lying. *Whatever Happened to the Human Race?*, with such an eminent physician as Dr. Koop as one of its guiding lights, made every effort to, and succeeded in, substantiating all of its claims. Its tone was informative, shunning the sensational tactics which characterize some of the abortion debate. (For example, Planned Parenthood has specialized in this regard in using proabortion ads that purport to present such "facts" as that, if abortion were outlawed, women would go to prison for having a miscarriage!) The film did carry a powerful message, but to accuse one's opponent of "propagandizing" simply for stating his case well is to indulge in propaganda oneself. The Religious Coalition for Abortion Rights' letter did exactly that.

[5]As an aside, one wonders at the self-respect any reporter can have who merely reads what some newspaper says and then reports it as fresh "news."

[6]From "The Myopic Press" in *Newsweek*, December 7, 1981.

[7]The exception being, of course, liberal theologians who are of the same tightly knit group merely dressed in religious raiments and therefore acceptable.

[8]Reminiscent of "as long as blacks lived in Africa . . ."

[9]E.g., the public (lack of) education system, one-and-a-half million abortions a year, crime rates so high as to be a virtual state of war,

child pornography, and all the other blessings we have that "just happen" to have come about as a "coincidence" with the demise of the Judaic-Christian ethic.

[10]"The Media As Present Danger" by Leopold Tyrmand, *The Rockford Papers*, Vol. 5, No. 4, September, 1980, p. 10.

[11]*Whatever Happened to the Human Race?* is a book-film series which I directed. It was launched with a twenty-city tour all across the USA, of which the New York seminar was one.

[12]One wonders how many murdered victims of terrorism would be alive today if the media had shown any self-restraint in their profitable manipulation of events which has turned much of the news into a poor man's Roman circus. *Newsweek* went so far as to call up Reagan's attempted assassin and give him a two-page interview.

Chapter 3

[1]Trappists take a lifelong vow of silence.

[2]*In Search of History: A Personal Adventure* (New York: Harper & Row, 1978), pp. 146, 147.

[3]For a complete statement of the Christian stand on the basis of principle against the state, read Francis Schaeffer's *A Christian Manifesto* (Westchester, Ill.: Crossway Books, 1981).

[4]Obviously, no mention is made of the thousands of restored lives: the drug addicts, alcoholics, criminals, who have been restored to human fullness and life by the influence of those "TV preachers."

Chapter 4

[1]Russ Pulliam wrote to me, "I beg you to tell people to get into journalism. How can we expect to change the views of the world if Christians won't even attempt to enter the media fields and change them from within"—to which I say Amen!

[2]As pointed out by John Whitehead in *The Second American Revolution*, British common law had a great deal to do with the foundation of American legal and political structures. Until recently William Blackstone, who was a lecturer at law at Oxford University, was studied by all law students, and anyone who had the vaguest interest in law, politics, and the constitutional process. He epitomized the British common law which was the basis for jurisprudence in the United States as well as Great Britain until the beginning of the twentieth century, when it was replaced by the absolutist intolerance of the Supreme Court and federal court system.

William Blackstone, who embodied the tenets of Judeo-Christian truth in his *Commentaries on the Laws of England,* published between 1765 and 1770, wrote: "Upon two foundations, the law of nature and the law of revelation, depend all human laws: that is to say, no human laws should be suffered to contradict these." Stated in a different way, William Blackstone, guiding light to our Founding Fathers in legal matters, clearly states that the laws of God take precedence over the dabblings of men.

Blackstone, through his writings, had a great influence on the men who founded American law and government. He confirmed through his writings that it was self-evident that God is the source of all law, whether laws are found in Holy Scripture or in nature. To Blackstone and the Founding Fathers, the very concept of "right," "law," "freedom," were meaningless without their divine origin. Thus, the very word "rights" conjured up the image of the Giver of rights. Otherwise, rights in themselves would be purely the whimsical arbitrary decisions of men (as indeed they are today because the idea of divine law has been abandoned).

³Charles Darwin's evolutionary theory, that man is *only* the product of "natural selection," with no divine intervention whatsoever, spread so rapidly because the church scorned it or ignored it, rather than pointing out its shortcomings. A completely materialistic interpretation of Darwinism deprives man of his sense of responsibility to his Creator and to other people and to the laws of the state. Darwinism tended to validate greed (i.e., if a businessman was exploiting his workers, he was doing so only because "nature" had "selected" him to be stronger and wiser). Pietists often took comfort in their religion on Sunday, and in their Darwinian bank accounts the rest of the week.

⁴In his monumental work on the deterioration of the Christian influence over the law and government in the United States, *The Second American Revolution,* John W. Whitehead, constitutional attorney, clearly points out that this myth of neutrality is indeed a cause for anger in the legal arena.

Statements by those such as Justice Hughes of the Supreme Court, he notes, illustrate the new view of the Constitution and the radical departure from the framers' intent. Justice Hughes said, "The Constitution is what the judges say it is." This view of law was in dire contrast to the traditional American concept of constitutionalism; that is, limited government under law.

Justice Felix Frankfurter also later parroted this view when he said, "It is they who speak [the Supreme Court justices] and not the Constitution."

This type of philosophy opened the door to the idea of evolution in the law and an evolving Constitution. Since man was seen as an evolving creature, it was only logical that his laws and customs should "evolve" with him.

Movement was mistaken for progress. What nobody seemed to notice was that the actual structure of the law, government and other branches of the system were moving backwards!

Justice Oliver Wendell Holmes, instrumental in introducing these inhuman ideas, actually went so far as to express the most crude Darwinian notion concerning the nature of man. Holmes said, "I see no reason for attributing to man a significance different in kind from that which belongs to a baboon or a grain of sand." With that view of the law, is it any wonder that Justice Holmes also said: "Truth is the majority vote of that nation that could lick all the others." This statement embodies, perhaps better than any other, the meaning of pure, arbitrary relativism. According to Holmes's logic, had Hitler won the war, he and the majority who backed him would have been morally right and had truth on their side.

All of these sentiments found their logical and horrifying conclusion in the abortion decision, which legalized the right of the "stronger" person to take the life of a defenseless infant.

This, in the same decade in which the "justice system" as a whole was unable to prevent a 20 percent rise in crime. Thus, while insisting on overly strict and sometimes petty rules of evidence, the law openly invites the death penalty to be applied to literally millions of innocent unborn. Schizophrenic? Sick? Yes, indeed, a time for anger!

[5]As an example, consider that Ronald Reagan, in spite of a prolife Republican platform in 1980, allowed the full funding of Planned Parenthood to go forward under his administration. Planned Parenthood receives a total of some seventy million federal dollars annually. A great amount of their activity is "public relations": the proabortion propaganda they distribute. (More about this later.) All of which enables them to devote their other funds to performing abortions. This from an administration voted into office by millions who favored a prolife stance. This in the same year when many other programs—school lunches and the like—were cut for budgetary reasons. A good statement of this is made in the following article:

> In the days following Mr. Reagan's election, liberal columnists urged the President-elect to abandon what were called social issues during the campaign. David Broder wrote that "efforts to legislate social behavior" would simply "squander [our] energies." Joseph Kraft derided them as "the Moral Majority's agenda." In the succeeding months, the treadmill of journalism reduced the term "social issues" to cartoonlike thinness. (Though Mr. Kraft conveniently forgets that in 1970 he wrote: "Let's face it, we reporters have very little to do with Middle America. They're not *our* kind of people.")
>
> The columnists should have had no fear. By now even Mr. Reagan seems to have come to the conclusion that the voters wanted from him only a repaired economy and a refurbished defense. He appears to have accepted the columnists' and pollsters' prognosis of what Middle America needs and wants.
>
> When it comes to voting, Middle America certainly understands the effect that unemployment, inflation and creeping pauperization have had on its paychecks and savings accounts. But to make economics the sole determining agent of voters is irresponsible. For the last 15 years Middle America has been in psychological chaos, bewildered at what has been happening to the non-economic dimension of its life.
>
> Middle America is neither a class nor a geographical notion. It exists in human consciousness in every corner of this land. Over the last 15 years, Middle America's fabric of beliefs, con-

ventions, norms, customs and moral values has been torn apart. As it happens, its cultural ethos has sustained Western civilization for two millennia, but no one was supposed to admit that. The new intellectual elite that was carrying out the process of demolition saw this as progress. During the 1970s, however, this assault got a little out of hand, even for some liberals.

Some fundamental perceptions of commonality and normality were being so thoroughly undermined that it became questionable whether a coherent social order could survive in the long run. An American presidency that chooses not to address itself to such a phenomenon risks being dismissed by history as weightless, its other achievements notwithstanding.

"Social issues" have always been in the purview of philosophers and moralists. It may come as an unpalatable surprise to many, but when one strips away much of the vulgar and unrefined rhetoric, what the Moral Majority wants is essentially what Moses and Christ proposed, what Plato and Aristotle dissected as ontological necessity, what St. Augustine, Aquinas, Dante and Maimonides endowed with sophistication, what Luther and Calvin imbued with moral passion.

A person who finds fundamentalists both physically and visually nauseating would be outraged to be told that they are direct descendants of 18th-Century common-sense intuitionism in philosophy and heirs to the millennia-old quandaries of the West's normative ethics. Those terms are not usually associated with the *Weltanschauung* of the car dealers and plumbers who respond to the Moral Majority's direct-mail campaigns. Such lineage naturally threatens the superior position taken by the Moral Majority's most ardent foes—the specific amalgam of journalists, scriptwriters, movie producers, politicians and publishers who feel threatened by the slightest mention of anything that might challenge their modern sitcom *cum* talk-show version of Sunday school.

It can be correctly said that there is little identification between the Moral Majority and Middle America's bodies of beliefs. Yet their concerns—moral and existential—seem to be the same, and the letters-to-the-editor sections of newspapers from coast to coast confirm such an assumption. Reading them, one quickly discovers that the code words for social issues—anti-abortionism, busing, school prayers, crime—have large, basic common denominators that can hardly be reduced to the term "social."

What preoccupies the Middle American mind—in countless simplifications—are problems of normality, sexual convention, retribution against vice and evil. Taken together, these issues form a sort of guideline for how to live and be rewarded for simple virtues—decency, fairness, compassion, responsibility before God, man and society—which have proved to be legitimate and functional through centuries of Western civilization.

Over the last century, some ideologies and sciences have dissolved the sense of evil and sin in modern man's mind. During our lifetime the interlocking system of Judeo-Christian notions and values has been relentlessly mocked. Questions about the human condition have dwindled in these climates to mere "issues." They have been demoted from the status of moral concern to the level of political action and legislation.

Many who voted for Mr. Reagan in 1980 thought something had to be said and done about it. Yet those who surround the President now seem to think there's no political profit in responding to that predicament. They appear uninterested in that blue-collar, Middle American voter who is essentially faithful to democratic recipes for economic well-being, but whose life has been invaded by the liberal culture that attached itself to the Democratic Party from 1960 onward. Before his election Ronald Reagan seemed to have an answer for them.

Now Mr. Reagan seems to be signaling that broadmindedness and tolerant compromise may be more appropriate. There's nothing wrong with broadmindedness and tolerance. One can admit as well that Aristotle's, Christ's, Dante's and Calvin's precepts may need to be revised according to what we know today about life, the world and society. The crucial question is, to what extent? How far should we stray away from rudimentary wisdom and well-tested truths? How many basic beliefs that have been transmuted into rational and moral tradition can we surrender without losing everything? The most common fallacy spread around by a hostile media is that Mr. Reagan's "simplism" and the Moral Majority's "bigotry" were determining the spirit of American conservatism and that Mr. Reagan obviously became wary of this kinship. In fact, it's the other way around: An intellectually complex and historically rich conservative doctrine was processed for political and popular use by both Mr. Reagan and the Moral Majority.

It is of course in the interest of liberal writers and editors who revile traditionalists and fundamentalists to persist in their supercilious attacks on the "social-issues" movement without according it a fair intellectual dialogue. And Washington's conservatives, bewitched by politics and economics, meekly acquiesce, unable to comprehend what the *New Republic* magazine so correctly perceived immediately after the 1980 election: "The vitality of the conservatives . . . owed a lot to the strength of their feelings on moral and cultural questions." (Leopold Tyrmand, "Washington Runs Away from the 'Social Issues,' " *Wall Street Journal,* April 29, 1982).

[6]As has been the case in the abortion on demand cases related to minors; i.e., in most states a minor cannot have her ears pierced

without parental consent, but can have the much more serious operation of abortion. Thus, the court not the parent becomes the final
authority and generator of the child's "rights."

[7]Nomination of Sandra Day O'Connor: Hearings Before The Committee On The Judiciary United States Senate, September 9, 10, and
11, 1981. Serial No. J-97-51, p. 60.

[8]The case was reported in the *Tulsa World*, Saturday, September 26,
1981; the *Daily Oklahoman*, Wednesday, October 7, 1981; and the
Tulsa World, Thursday, October 1981. Here are the details:

The following is a detailed chronological account of the recent
Oklahoma City District Court case involving a twelve-year-old girl
who became pregnant allegedly as the result of a rape by three boys of
the ages of 16-17 years. The girl also contracted gonorrhea, allegedly
from the rape. The court first ordered an abortion, but subsequently
vacated that order.

The twelve-year-old girl first ran away from home and subsequently was detained in Berry House, a detention center in Oklahoma City
for juveniles. While at Berry House, it was discovered that the girl
was pregnant and had gonorrhea. Her account of being gang-raped
was then first learned of. Proceedings were then instituted in the
Juvenile Division of the Oklahoma County District Court to have the
girl adjudicated a "Deprived Child" pursuant to Title 10 Oklahoma
Statutes Section 1101(d), so that an abortion could be performed and
paid for by the Department of Human Services of the State of Oklahoma.

At the initial hearing in the juvenile court, the twelve-year-old girl
was represented by the Public Defender's office of Oklahoma County. The girl's mother (a member of the Church of the Holiness), who
objected to the abortion on moral and religious grounds, was subsequently represented by Mrs. Michelle Porta, a private attorney,
appointed by the presiding Special District Judge Donald Manning.

At the initial hearing, a letter from a private physician, referred to as
Dr. A, was introduced as medical evidence in support of the girl
having an abortion. In that report, which is now inaccessible since the
file is closed by statute, Dr. A allegedly stated that the girl, who
reportedly wanted the abortion, was in a life-threatening situation due
to the pregnancy. The abortion would have to be performed immediately since the girl was approaching the end of the first trimester.

It was then ordered by Judge Manning that an abortion should be
performed on the girl, as he found the girl's life "endangered by the
pregnancy," but the judge stayed the order to allow an appeal by the
mother to the State Supreme Court on the question of whether an
abortion should be performed on the girl as a "deprived child." It is
notable that the judge's order simply ordered that the pregnancy be
terminated and contained no provision for vacating the order in the
event the girl withdrew her consent to an abortion.

Judge Manning also instructed the mother of the child not to discuss with her daughter whether or not the latter should have the abortion and apparently instructed the girl not to discuss the matter with her mother. Such orders are unprecedented in American jurisprudence.

Upon the appeal to the Supreme Court, the matter was heard by the said Court within a couple of days. Mrs. Porta, the mother's attorney, was given "two hours" notice of oral arguments in the Court. Five days after Judge Manning's order of September 23, 1981, the Supreme Court filed an order signed by the Chief Justice affirming the trial court's order.

The abortion was then scheduled for the following Monday morning by an abortionist in Norman, Oklahoma. In the meantime, the twelve-year-old girl changed her mind and stated that she did not want an abortion, but wanted to carry the child to term. It was at this point that Rep. Bill Graves entered the case as co-counsel for the mother at Mrs. Porta's and the mother's request. The mother's attorneys then went to the courthouse at 8:30 A.M. Monday morning and informed the judge of the young girl's change of mind.

Judge Manning then ordered an *in camera* hearing at which the twelve-year-old girl and her mother both testified. The girl testified that she no longer wanted the abottion, but wanted her child to be born. The girl gave as her reason that it was morally wrong to have an abortion. She also testified that while at Berry House, someone there told her that the only way the court would let her leave Berry House and go home was if she consented to an abortion. In regard to this charge, Judge Manning (who made no such requirement) at a subsequent hearing stated he had the matter investigated and was satisfied that no one at Berry House had told the girl such a thing.

The judge then interrogated the girl and her mother as to whether they had discussed between themselves as to whether or not the girl should have the abortion. They both said "no." An *in camera* discussion was then had between the judge and the attorneys (the girl and mother having departed), the latter of whom included Mrs. Porta and Mr. Graves, the Assistant Public Defender and an Assistant District Attorney. Both the latter were distressed over the fact that they feared "prolife" people had gotten hold of the girl and caused her to change her mind. The Assistant District Attorney was also distressed over the possibility of the matter being decided on religious grounds. An attorney for the mother then interjected that he hoped all concerned had not reached the state where a girl could not utilize her own moral values in making a decision to have an abortion or not. The same attorney then suggested that since it was quite obvious that the twelve-year-old girl had been examined and influenced by proabortion doctors prior to her initial decision to have the abortion, it was only fair that she be examined and counseled also by prolife doctors.

Judge Manning then announced that he was going to have an expert in obstetrics selected by the Oklahoma Medical Association examine the girl and advise the court whether or not she should have the abortion. Dr. B, an expert obstetrician who is proabortion, was elected. The girl was then examined by Dr. B.

Shortly thereafter, a hearing was held at which Dr. B, Dr. A and Dr. A's superior all testified. All admitted at the hearing that they were proabortion. However, Dr. B testified that since the girl did not want an abortion and her life was not threatened by the pregnancy, she should not have an abortion. When asked to elaborate, Dr. B said that he could just not visualize "taking a twelve-year-old girl kicking and screaming" down to the abortionist when she did not want an abortion.

Dr. B also testified that the risk to the girl's life in having the child was hardly more than that to the average adult woman and that it was possible she could have the child by natural birth rather than cesarean. He also indicated that his examination had revealed that the girl no longer had gonorrhea and that the past presence of the disease was not a danger in any way to the unborn child or the girl. On cross-examination of Dr. B, the Assistant District Attorney attempted to elicit testimony from the obstetrician to the effect that it would be better for the girl to have the abortion. However, Dr. B would not be deterred from his position that the girl should not have the abortion.

Dr. A then got on the stand and stated her concurrence in the position of Dr. B. She also said that her previous statement concerning a "life-threatening" situation was meant in a "general way" and not as to the 12-year-old girl in particular. If that was the case, it is possible the court was misled by Dr. A's report. The court's finding that the girl's life was endangered had to be based on that report since it was the only medical evidence the court had on which to base its order for the abortion. Dr. A also admitted that she is proabortion.

Dr. C, also proabortion, then testified that he was Dr. A's superior and that he subscribed to the opinion of Dr. B that there should not be an abortion in this case.

The twelve-year-old girl then was called to the stand and reiterated that she no longer wanted the abortion. She also repeated her earlier charge in which she testified that someone at Berry House had told her that the only way the court would let her leave Berry House and go home was if she consented to the abortion. She later told Bill Graves that Dr. A had told her that her life was endangered if she had the child.

It is remarkable that during her testimony, the Assistant Public Defender Jeanne Bauman, who was officially there to represent the girl, asked the girl if she realized that if she had the child it could cause economic hardship to her and her family. These questions were successfully objected to and prevented on the grounds of intimidation and coercion.

On completion of testimony Judge Manning vacated his order for an abortion and dismissed the case.

It was later charged by Jeanne Bauman that the girl had withdrawn consent to an abortion after being influenced by prolife forces (apparently meaning Rep. Graves who is known locally as a prolife proponent). However, Graves said he did not enter the case until after the girl had changed her mind.

It is remarkable that the court made a finding that the girl was a "deprived child" due to needing an abortion since the statute (10 O.S. 1101[d]) does not include such a classification. Subsection d does define "deprived child" in part as a child "in need of special care and treatment because of his physical or mental condition" whose parents are unable or unwilling to provide for him or her. However, the same subsection also provides:

> ". . . no child who, in good faith, is being provided with treatment and care by spiritual means alone in accordance with the tenets and practice of a recognized church or religious denomination by a duly accredited practitioner thereof shall, for that reason alone, be considered to be a deprived child under any provision of this act."

The foregoing, since the mother objected to the abortion on religious grounds, would seem to have been sufficient reason for the court not to declare the twelve-year-old girl a "deprived child." However, there is no indication that the aforementioned religious clause was considered in this case.

Apparently the above provision was not brought to the court's attention.

[9]*Los Angeles Daily Journal,* Oct. 27, 1981; *Los Angeles Daily Journal,* Oct. 21, 1981. (In addition, local newspaper coverage and national television and radio spot.)

[10]Out of the one million five hundred thousand abortions performed every year "legally" in the United States, it is estimated that 6 percent, in other words 90,000 of them, occur after twenty-four weeks when, even by the courts' standards, life is viable.

[11]As quoted in the *Catholic League's Newsletter,* January, 1982, Vol. 9, No. 1.

Chapter 5

[1]Even in the United States, eugenics polluted our history by the forcible sterilization of sixty thousand people before 1960 under the Immigration Act of 1924.

[2]See *The Ultimate Resource* by Julian L. Simon (Princeton: Princeton University Press, 1982) for a totally contrary view on resources to the popular "We're running out, let's kill people" idea.

[3]The *Wall Street Journal,* Wednesday, September 2, 1981.

[4]Neutral? Planned Parenthood of Washington, D.C., named February 14-21, 1982, NATIONAL CONDOM WEEK. This year's Condom Week had the distinct honor of being made official by Mayor Marion Barry through one of his mayoral proclamations.

Included among the celebrations of National Condom week were:

> A symposium on Male Sexuality, a talk on Male Contraception, and last but not least, an evening of enjoyment and educational exchange called . . . RUBBER DISCO!
>
> Yes, it is the 4th annual RUBBER DISCO. Admission is free with a condom and an invitation which can be picked up at the men's Center of Planned·Parenthood (located at 1108 16th Street, NW—that is, 16th and L). This fabulous dance will be held at The Beret discotheque, decorated with a rainbow of different colored, blown up condoms. The height of festivities will culminate with a condom blowing contest, the winner of which is to receive a prize of $35.00.

(Source: A promotional letter mailed from Planned Parenthood and signed by Paula Wilborne, the Community Liaison of the National Condom Week Task Force, and fliers which accompanied it. Also, details about the dance itself were obtained by calling Planned Parenthood.)

Chapter 6

[1]First and foremost, when discussing the myth of neutrality in science and medicine and the incredible holocaust of death that this myth has brought upon us through abortion and infanticide, I must refer the reader to the book, *Whatever Happened to the Human Race?* (Old Tappan, NJ: Revell, 1979). Anyone with the least desire to understand the problems facing Christians and those with Judeo-Christian principles today should read and study that book.

[2]At least he cannot plead ignorance.

[3]Provine also forgets to mention that the "big bang" theory, which recent discoveries by astronomers tend to confirm, holds that the universe began at a definite and sudden point of time, and that therefore, since something had to cause the explosion, a being or force must have done so; and this utterly coincides with the Genesis account of creation. (See *God and the Astronomers* by the renowned Robert Jastrow.)

[4]See Francis Schaeffer, *How Should We Then Live?* (Old Tappan, NJ: Revell, 1976) for more on this topic.

[5]New euphemism—remember "final solution"?

[6]Upjohn is located in Kalamazoo, Michigan. Their address is: 3651 Van Rick Drive, Kalamazoo, MI 49001. (My note.)

[7]The Turks began the century with the first attempt at "modern" genocide of the Armenians. They had to resort to such crudities as throwing babies into the air and catching them on their bayonets. What a fine testimony to progress that by the end of the same century we will, thanks to Upjohn, be able to accomplish the same ends with a suppository!

[8]In our film *Whatever Happened to the Human Race?* we said much the same thing *as a warning*. Some thought it "farfetched." Let them read Provine to see that what we offered as a warning, he proffers with positive anticipation!

Chapter 7

[1]Here is an article that appeared in *The Wall Street Journal,* Monday, April 12, 1982, titled "Parents, Schools and Values Clarification" by Richard A. Baer, Jr., an associate professor in the department of natural resources at New York State College of Agriculture and Life Sciences, Cornell Uniersity.

Back in the mid-1960s, social scientists Louis E. Raths, Merrill Harmin and Sidney B. Simon developed the teaching method known as Values Clarification, advertising it as an ideal way to deal with values without taking sides or indoctrinating students in one particular value position. Since "by definition and right . . . values are personal things" ("Values and Teaching," 1966), teachers should never try to teach children correct values. To tell a student stealing is wrong or that kindness and loyalty are good values, would be, according to Values Clarification, to manipulate and coerce a student. Teachers should help students discover and clarify their own personal values instead of trying to force someone else's values on them.

Spread by teacher workshops, paid for in part by state and federal tax dollars, Values Clarification caught on quickly in the early 1970s and became popular with many teachers and adminisrators. Its use in public school sex-education classes and by local Planned Parenthood groups was particlarly noteworthy, for whether intended or not, adolescents were in effect given the message that parents, the school or society had no right to tell them what standards should guide sexual behavior. Whether premarital sex was right or wrong, for instance, adolescents would discover for themselves as they were helped to clarify their personal values.

Parents did not react immediately. But when children began to report over dinner that class discussion had been about whether lying was sometimes permissible and whether they should always obey their parents, it wasn't long before groups of parents began to mobilize against Values Clarification.

Emotions Outstripped Logic

Many of these parents were Christian fundamentalits. Their arguments were not couched in the sophisticated jargon of philosophy or social science, and sometimes emotions outstripped logic. But they left little doubt that they thought Values Clarification was teaching their children a kind of ethical relativism.

Instead of meeting such objections with solid arguments of their own, many educators attacked the objectors, dismissing their criticisms as little more than a reactionary fundamentalist response to education innovation.

This is precisely what happened, for example, in the spring of 1979 in a dispute over Values Clarification in the consolidated school system of Spencer and Van Etten, two small Upstate New York communities not far from Elmira. Supporters of Values Clarification referred early in the conflict to the concerned parents as simplistic, anti-intellectual and opposed to independent thought. One teacher accused them of having ties with national right-wing groups. But what was most embarrassing about this dispute was that it soon became apparent to several outside observers (including myself) that these "anti-intellectual" parents had a better grasp of the philosophical issues involved than the professional educators.

Martin Eger, professor of philosophy and physics at the City University of New York, pointed out in a spring 1981 article in the *Public Interest* that the climate of trust eroded rapidly after the school at first denied the Values Clarification made up any part of the required curriculum. When it became public knowledge that it did form the basis of at least one required course in vocational decision-making, school authorities still refused to meet in open, mediated dialogue with the protesters. The parents were left with no recourse but to accept the use of Values Clarification—which they thought would violate their consciences—or attempt a political solution by entering their own candidates in school board elections.

The basic complaints of the parents in Spencer-Van Etten and in many similar cases have now been largely substantiated. Over the past seven years, nonfundamentalist scholars from major universities—including professors Kenneth A. Strike of Cornell, Alan L. Lockwood of the University of Wisconsin and John S. Stewart, formerly of Michigan State University—have faulted Values Clarification on at least a dozen counts. The list of critics also includes William J. Bennett, recently appointed by President Reagan as chairman of the National Endowment for the Humanities, and Edwin J. Delattre, president of St. John's College in Annapolis. The major objections of these writers are virtually identical with those initially raised by religious fundamentalits and other parents' groups.

First, contrary to what its proponents claim, Values Clarification is not values-neutral. Even on the level of particular ethical decisions, where the authors try hard to be neutral, they succeed only partially. As Messrs. Bennett and Delattre point out, the approach used in such Values Clarification strategies as Sidney Simon's "Priorities" "emphatically indoctrinates—by encouraging and even exhorting the student to narcissistic self-gratification."

And on the deeper level of what philosophers call

"metaethics"—that is, critical analysis and theory about the nature of values as such—the claim to neutrality is entirely misleading. At this more basic level, the originators of Values Clarification simply assume that their own subjectivist theory of values is correct. By affirming the complete relativity of all values, they in effect equate values with personal tastes and preferences. If parents object to their children using pot or engaging in premarital sex, the theory behind Values Clarification makes it appropriate for the child to respond, "But that's just *your* value judgment. Don't force it on me."

Furthermore, Values Clarification indoctrinates students in ethical relativism, for its proponents push their own position on their captive student audiences and never suggest that thoughtful people may choose alternatives. Sidney Simon, Howard Kirschenbaum and other Values Clarification authors repeatedly belittle teachers of traditional values. Such teachers, they claim, "moralize," "preach," "manipulate" and "whip the child into line." Their positions are "rigid" and they rely on "religion and other cultural truisms."

The second major fault, according to the University of Wisconsin's Alan Lockwood, is that "a substantial proportion of the content and methods of Values Clarification constitutes a threat to the privacy rights of students and their families." To be sure, the method permits students to say "I pass" when the teacher asks them to complete such open-ended sentences as "If I had 24 hours to live . . .", "Secretly I wish . . ." or "My parents are usually. . . ." But many of these "projective techniques" are designed in such a fashion, Mr. Lockwood claims, that students often will realize too late that they have divulged more about themselves and their families than they wish or feel is appropriate in a public setting. Moreover, the method itself incorporates pressure toward self-disclosure.

Contradicting the Bible

A third criticism of Values Clarification is that by presupposing very specific views about human nature and society, it becomes a kind of "religious" position in its own right which competes directly with other religious views. For instance, Values Clarification theory consistently presents the individual self as the final arbiter of value truth (individuals must develop their own values "out of personal choices"), and it assumes that the good life is one of self-fulfillment and self-actualization. These positions directly contradict the Biblical view that God is the ultimate lawgiver and that the good life is to be found only in losing oneself in the service of God and of one's neighbor.

The use of Values Clarification in public schools or even by such quasi-public agencies as Planned Parenthood constitutes a direct violation of First Amendment protection against the establishment of religion, one at least as objectionable as the attempt by some fundamentalists to require the teaching of creationism in the public schools. Schools that use the method are, probably unwittingly, fostering the establishment of one particular "religion" and by doing so are abusing the rights of those who hold differing positions.

The controversy over Values Clarification tells us something about the quality of public discourse in this country. The educational establishment and the press ought to recognize that there is as much diversity among religious fundamentalists as among Catholics, Jews and liberal Protestants. Gratuitous sniping against blacks, women, Jews, Chicanos and Roman Catholics is no longer tolerated, but somehow fundamentalists who speak out against a development like Value Clarification remain fair game for the worst kinds of prejudicial attack. A bit more fairness is long overdue.

[2] The *Wall Street Journal,* February 22, 1982.

[3] Personal letter from Harold Fickett to the author.

[4] In some circles, having a child as a sort of proof of fertility to the sterile feminist has resurfaced as a respectably fashionable gesture. One can only suppose that when the novelty wears off, the child will be abandoned to a day-care center, or worse.

[5] From the Book of Isaiah, Chapters 1 through 6.

[6] As quoted in the *Wall Street Journal.*

Chapter 8

[1] In literature alone, T. S. Eliot, W. H. Auden, Graham Greene, Francois Mauriac, George Bernanos, J. R. R. Tolkien, C. S. Lewis, Flannery O'Connor, Solzhenitsyn, Walker Percy and many others have written. More recently there have been new younger writers like Larry Woiwode who have emerged.

[2] Christian books, especially nonfiction, often sell in excess of 250,000 copies in the first year after publication.

[3] Personal correspondence to the author.

[4] When half a million Christians (Washington for Jesus) converged on Washington, D.C., the event was relegated to minimal coverage at best. The next day eight hundred to twelve hundred lesbians marched in Washington and, by contrast, received Page One coverage.

[5] Sometimes not so "subtle," either. No group has been more active in trying to remove, censor and suppress books than the feminists. They are even carrying on a rewrite of the Bible itself.

[6] Note, however, that this film was not made by Christians and reflected Christian content merely because of the integrity of those involved in following the original true story.

[7] In the end, my talks with Bach came to nothing because he was fired after Michael Cimino's failure with *Heaven's Gate.*

Appendix

[1] From the *Philadelphia Inquirer,* August 2, 1981.

Suggestions for Further Reading

Reference Works

Andrew, Brother, *The Ethics of Smuggling*. Wheaton, IL: Tyndale House, 1975.

Hitchcock, James, *What Is Secular Humanism?* Ann Arbor, MI: Servant Books, 1982.

Jackson, Jeremy, *No Other Foundation: The Church Through Twenty Centuries*. Westchester, IL: Crossway Books, 1980.

Koop, C. Everett, *Right to Live; Right to Die*. Wheaton, IL: Tyndale House, 1976.

Mander, Jerry, *Four Arguments for the Elimination of Television*. New York: Morrow, 1978.

Peters, Charles, *How Washington Really Works*. Reading, MA: Addison-Wesley, 1980.

Schaeffer, Francis A., *A Christian Manifesto*. Westchester, IL: Crossway Books, 1981.

Schaeffer, Francis A., *The Complete Works of Francis A. Schaeffer*. Westchester, IL: Crossway Books, 1982. Contains all of Francis Schaeffer's books, including those mentioned in this list.

Schaeffer, Francis A., and Koop, C. Everett, *Whatever Happened to the Human Race?* Old Tappan, NJ: Revell, 1976.

Schaeffer, Franky, *Addicted to Mediocrity*. Westchester, IL: Crossway Books, 1981.

Shirer, William, *The Rise and Fall of the Third Reich*. New York: Simon & Schuster, 1981.

Simon, Julian L., *The Ultimate Resource*. Princeton, NJ: Princeton Press, 1981.

Sobel, Robert, *The Manipulation*. Garden City, NY: Doubleday, 1976.

Whitehead, John W., *The Second American Revolution*. Elgin, IL: David C. Cook, 1982.

Magazines and Journals

The Chalcedon Report (P.O. Box 158, Vallecito, CA 95251).

Commentary Magazine (165 E. 56th Street, New York, NY 10022).

Debate Magazine (P.O. Box 11796, Ft. Lauderdale, FL 33306).

The Rockford Papers (Rockford Institute, Rockford, IL 61111).

Novels

I suggest you read or reread these works of fiction to better place our moment of history.

Bayly, Joseph, *Winterflight*. Waco, TX: Word, 1981.

Bradbury, Ray, *Fahrenheit 451*. New York: Simon & Schuster, 1967.

Burgess, Anthony, *A Clockwork Orange*. New York: Norton, 1963.

Huxley, Aldous, *Brave New World*. New York: Harper and Row, 1932, 1979 paper.

Lewis, C. S., *C. S. Lewis Space Trilogy: Out of the Silent Planet, Perelandra, That Hideous Strength*. New York: Macmillan, 1943, 1968, 1968 respectively. See especially *That Hideous Strength*.

Orwell, George, *Animal Farm*. New York: New American Library, 1974.

Orwell, George, *1984*. New York: New American Library, 1971.

Tolkien, J. R. R., *The Lord of the Rings: Fellowship of the Ring, The Two Towers, The Return of the King*. Boston: Houghton Mifflin, 1974.

Films

In the documentary vein, several of the films with which I have been associated would be very helpful to an individual or group working through these problems. Most of them are available for rent from Gospel Films in Muskegon, Michigan (1-800-253-0413).

How Should We Then Live? (10 episodes).

Reclaiming the World (Conversations with Francis and Edith Schaeffer) (10 episodes).

The Second American Revolution (one film; for information write to Franky Schaeffer V Productions, Inc., P.O. Box 909, Los Gatos, CA 95031).

Whatever Happened to the Human Race? (5 episodes).

The above resources form a very limited list of possible reading and viewing to stimulate further thought on the topics covered in this book. However, they will serve as a start.